C0 BPX 641

ROBERT BOYLE

A Study in Science and Christian Belief

R. Hooykaas

With a Foreword by

John Hedley Brooke
Michael Hunter

The Pascal Centre for Advanced Studies in Faith and Science
Redeemer College, Ancaster, Ontario
and
University Press of America, Inc.
Lanham • New York • Oxford

BT
1117
.H6
1997

Copyright © 1997 by
University Press of America,® Inc.
4720 Boston Way
Lanham, Maryland 20706

12 Hid's Copse Rd.
Cummor Hill, Oxford OX2 9JJ

All rights reserved
Printed in the United States of America
British Library Cataloguing in Publication Information Available

Copublished by arrangement with
The Pascal Centre for Advanced Studies in Faith and Science

Library of Congress Cataloging-in-Publication Data

Hooykaas, R. (Reijer)
Robert Boyle : a study in science and Christian belief / by R.
Hooykaas; with a foreword by John Hedley Brooke and Michael
Hunter.
    p.   cm.
Includes bibliographical references and index.
1. Boyle, Robert, 1627-1691--Religion. 2. Apologetics--England--
History--17th century 3. Religion and science--England--History--
17th century. I. Title.
    BT1117.H66   1997   192--dc21   97-3491 CIP

ISBN 0-7618-0708-X (cloth: alk. ppr.)

⊖™ The paper used in this publication meets the minimum
requirements of American National Standard for information
Sciences—Permanence of Paper for Printed Library Materials,
ANSI Z39.48—1984

The Pascal Centre, established in 1988 by Redeemer College, specializes in studies of the relationship between faith and science from a biblical perspective. The Centre intends to encourage an open-minded discussion of issues in faith and science from this perspective. However, the opinions expressed in this book are strictly those of the author and contributors and do not necessarily represent the Pascal Centre or Redeemer College.

The Pascal Centre for Advanced Studies in Faith and Science
Redeemer College
777 Highway 53 East, Ancaster, Ontario
Canada L9K 1J4

TABLE OF CONTENTS

FOREWORD

With the death of Reijer Hooykaas in January 1994, the world of scholarship lost an eminent historian of science, whose understanding of the relations between Reformation theology and the early scientific movement retains a distinctive place in the historiography of the "Scientific Revolution." From 1945 to 1966 Hooykaas held the Chair of History of Science in the Free University at Amsterdam, combining it with a Professorship in Mineralogy from 1948 to 1960. He subsequently occupied the Chair of History of Science at Utrecht from 1967 to 1976. In a recent book, dedicated to his memory, H. Floris Cohen not only records his personal debt to Hooykaas but identifies a theme recurrent in his writings: science, rightly understood, teaches the lesson of humility.[1] Describing himself as an old-fashioned Calvinist[2] Hooykaas would draw parallels, as Francis Bacon did in the seventeenth century, between humility before God's Word and humility before His Works,[3] both prerequisites of the Christian philosopher.

For Hooykaas this was a parallel that could illuminate our understanding of the scientific movement in early modern Europe because, in his view, the most singular deficiency in Greek philosophizing about nature had been its lack of a disciplined empiricism, a certain blindness to the possibility of "facts" that might slay a beautiful theory. If a greater reverence for the facts of nature was a precondition of modern science, Hooykaas was impressed by three developments in the cultural history of Europe which helped to achieve it. The most distant of these was the famous decree of 1277 in which Etienne Tempier had condemned the dogmatism enshrined within numerous Aristotelian propositions. A truly omnipotent deity could not be bound by what

---

[1] H. Floris Cohen, *The Scientific Revolution-A Historiographical Inquiry* (Chicago: University of Chicago Press, 1994), 356f.

[2] See the obituary notice by Oliver R. Barclay in *Science and Christian Belief* 6 (1994): 129–32.

[3] Reijer Hooykaas, "The Christian Approach in Teaching Science," *Science and Christian Belief* 6 (1994): 113–28 (originally published in 1960).

Aristotle had deemed necessarily to be the case in the structure of the cosmos. In subsequent voluntarist theologies of Creation, an emphasis on the freedom of God to make whatever world He wished encouraged a sense of the contingency of nature, for the study of which empirical rather than *a priori* methods were appropriate. On this point Hooykaas aligned himself with the conclusions of the Cambridge philosopher Michael Foster who, during the 1930s, had ascribed the limitations of Greek science to an inadequate theology of nature.[4] The second of the three developments to which Hooykaas attached importance was more down to earth: the voyages of discovery launched by the Portuguese, which falsified Ptolemy's *Geography* and such common wisdom as the existence of a torrid zone that was impassable and uninhabitable. Finally there was the Reformation itself, which constituted a challenge to authority in the religious and political spheres that could find comparable expression in a revolt against the authority of Aristotle in the domain of natural philosophy. Hooykaas knew only too well that Protestants could be as reactionary as Catholics in matters of natural philosophy, but he insisted on certain trends in the progress of the Reformation that would catalyze the serious study of nature. One was a re-evaluation of manual work that helped to meet one of Bacon's desiderata for the reform of learning: the removal of social barriers between scholar and craftsman. Another was the doctrine of biblical accommodation, as developed by Calvin. By stressing that the language of Scripture was not to be deemed authoritative on scientific technical-ities because it had been accommodated to the needs of the unlearned, space was created for the admission of novelties, such as the Coperni-can innovation, which proved so difficult for the Catholic Church to accept. Hooykaas would also speak of a "biblical worldview," which he believed had a beneficial effect on European science by purging the natural world of a vestigial pantheism—cleansing it of quasi-intelligent agents which, in terms of Calvin's theology, detracted from divine sovereignty. What Hooykaas meant by the biblical worldview was one in which causal efficacy resided not within nature but ultimately in a transcendent God who had prescribed "rules" for His creation—rules

---

[4] For a discussion of Foster's analysis, see Cameron Wybrow, ed., *Creation, Nature and Political Order in the Philosophy of Michael Foster (1903–1959): The Classic* Mind *Articles and Others, with Modern Critical Essays* (Lampeter: Edwin Mellon Press, 1992). And for an instructive review: David Bloor, "The Moving Forces of History," *British Journal for the History of Science* 27 (1994): 351–55.

which some thinkers would call the laws of nature and which were open to empirical investigation.

It might be inferred from such remarks that Hooykaas was content to present the "Scientific Revolution" as the simple triumph of empiricism over metaphysics and ancient wisdom. This would, however, be a travesty of his position because he recognized that the de-personalization of "nature" which, in the seventeenth century, went along with what he called its "de-deification" found expression in a new metaphysics that has come to be known as the "mechanical philosophy." Natural phenomena that had once been ascribed to final causes, to hidden powers of affinity and antipathy or to substantial "forms" were increasingly (though by no means exclusively) attributed to the arrangement and motion of colorless, microscopic particles. In the clockwork universe of Descartes the real world ceased to be the world as perceived. The workings of nature lay hidden behind appearances (behind the clock face, as it were) and could only be grasped by the construction of mechanical models. This demand for intelligible mechanical explanation did not always sit comfortably with a demand for empirical demonstration; but one philosopher who tried to hold them together was Robert Boyle, whose enthusiasm for chemistry appears to have derived in part from his belief that it could supply experimental support for a mechanical philosophy that he considered excellent both in its own right and for its theological implications. Through chemistry, art could imitate nature, a possibility newly sanctioned by the assimilation of nature itself to man-made machinery.

With a deep personal interest in each of these themes, and having been, in the first instance, a historian of chemistry, one can understand why Hooykaas was particularly drawn to Boyle for one of his first major studies. Many of his later books and papers have appeared in English. Indeed his *Religion and the Rise of Modern Science*, first published by Scottish Academic Press in 1972, was used during the 1970s as a set text for an Open University course entitled *Science and Belief from Copernicus to Darwin*. Consequently several generations of students encountered one of the clearest statements of what Rolf Gruner has described as the "revisionist" thesis—that there were auspicious interconnections between the Protestant Reformation and the expansion of science.[5] Despite Gruner's objections, it is a thesis that has resurfaced in the work of other historians of science, notably in Colin

---

[5] Rolf Gruner, "Science, Nature and Christianity," *Journal of Theological Studies* 26 (1975): 55–81.

Russell's *Cross Currents*.[6] Also available in English have been those important studies of nineteenth-century science in which Hooykaas analyzed the conventional antithesis between "uniformitarianism" and "catastrophism" in the historical sciences, arguing that there had been catastrophists in geology who deserved better than routine caricature and secular derision.[7] The need for a re-evaluation was confirmed when Martin Rudwick exposed the inadequacy of William Whewell's original categories.[8] Writers on these issues today still speak of a massive debt to Hooykaas,[9] and to Susan Cannon who shared his conviction that the supposed "uniformitarian-catastrophist debate" could not be reduced to the triumph of modernity over religious bias.[10]

İt is a fitting tribute to Hooykaas that his close study of Boyle's published writings should now enjoy an English translation. Written under the dark cloud of the Nazi occupation, it has hitherto been accessible only through an original and rare Dutch edition, to which both author and translator refer in their respective Notes. To read this text for the first time is to be reminded of the insight and authority that Hooykaas could command through his intensive analysis of primary sources. We find him renouncing the common view that Boyle had given an essentially modern definition of a chemical element. He writes with a real sympathy for his subject, responding to the piety that Boyle expressed in his published works. One even senses that Hooykaas found in Boyle the perfect exemplification (perhaps in certain respects the foundation) of a historiography in which mutual reinforcement (rather

---

[6] Colin A. Russell, *Cross-Currents: Interactions Between Science and Faith* (Leicester: Inter-Varsity Press, 1985).

[7] Reijer Hooykaas, *The Principle of Uniformity in Geology, Biology and Theology* (Leiden: Brill, 1963); *Catastrophism, Its Scientific Character in Relation to Actualism and Uniformitarianism* (Amsterdam: North-Holland Publishing Co., 1970).

[8] Martin J. S. Rudwick, "Uniformity and Progression: Reflections on the Structure of Geological Theory in the Age of Lyell," in *Perspectives in the History of Science and Technology*, ed. Duane H. D. Roller (Norman: University of Oklahoma Press, 1971), 209–27.

[9] See, for example, M. J. S. Hodge, "The History of the Earth, Life and Man: Whewell and Palaetiological Science," in *William Whewell: A Composite Portrait*, ed. Menachem Fisch and Simon Schaffer (Oxford: Oxford University Press, 1991), 255–88, at p. 256.

[10] Susan (originally Walter) F. Cannon, "The Uniformitarian–Catastrophist Debate," *Isis* 51 (1960): 38–55; *Science in Culture: The Early Victorian Period* (Folkestone: Dawson, 1978).

than opposition) between science and religion would be stressed. In his finely tuned comparison between Boyle and Descartes, there is reference to that banishing of all immaterial agents from physical explanation, for which he later used the term "de-deification." In Boyle's critique of "vulgar" conceptions of a personified Nature Hooykaas found vivid proof that the metaphysical foundations of the mechanical philosophy were theistic, not naturalistic: the "rules" of nature to which Boyle referred were emphatically God-given, sustained by divine power and subject to over-ruling in the case of the biblical miracles.[11] In Boyle, Hooykaas found explicit claims for the imitation of nature—in the manner, for example, in which the chemist might make artificial gems. This undermining of the nature/art distinction was to be a prominent theme in *Religion and the Rise of Modern Science.*[12] Boyle's retention (in contradistinction to Descartes) of the design argument for God's existence is given a sympathetic exposition in keeping with Hooykaas' insistence that, for Boyle, natural theology was not independent of, but a form of, revealed religion. It was also a defense of revealed religion in a period which had seen Christian sects proliferate so greatly that a visit to London might well deprive a man of his faith: this was Boyle's own observation in letters of 1646 and 1647, to which Hooykaas drew attention in his section on "Scripture and the Confessions." Hooykaas clearly had respect for a thinker whose defense of Christianity against the atheists and materialists of his day would have "challenged even a nineteenth-century materialist."[13] Many times in the text we are shown that association of humility with empiricism which Hooykaas saw as a mainspring of the scientific movement. As he put it in chapter 2: "the greatest respect is paid to the facts"; and again: "what experiments cannot decide Boyle leaves undecided, implying a considerable restriction of his rationalism." When, in *The Excellency of Theology*, Boyle observed that "There is scarce any sort of learned men, that is more apt to undervalue those that are versed only in other parts of knowledge, than many of our modern naturalists," he launched a critique of scientism with which Hooykaas clearly empathized. In the closing sections of the text that empathy becomes tangible. There is reference to Boyle's "evangelical piety," "strict morality" and "affinity with the Low Church." Boyle's deference

---

[11] The affinity with Hooykaas's own theology can be seen in "The Christian Approach in Teaching Science" (n. 3), 122–24.

[12] Reijer Hooykaas, *Religion and the Rise of Modern Science* (Edinburgh: Scottish Academic Press, 1972), 54–71.

[13] See Hooykaas' own Introduction to the text.

to the Bible and to what Hooykaas calls the "fundamental principles of
the Reformation" are thrown into sharp relief.

This is not to suggest that Hooykaas simply created a Boyle in his
own image. It is clear from the text that he could be censorious when
he found Boyle too cautious in his science, too weak in the analogies
he deployed (as when he compared divine activity in nature with the
ability of the human mind to govern the body), and too spare in his
theology, as when he missed the point that "acceptance of special
revelation (Scripture) requires a special grace, just as general revelation
in nature is accepted by a general or common grace." In such remarks,
however, Hooykaas' theological preferences are made clear. Because
he made no secret of his belief that the history of science was a potent
(perhaps the most potent) resource for teaching evangelical Christian
attitudes towards science, his historical writings have sometimes been
criticized for the theological freight they carried. This is always a
sensitive issue when evaluating the work of those who write on the
mutual bearings of scientific and religious discourse. One cannot deny
that Calvin had a higher profile in *Religion and the Rise of Modern
Science* than in most accounts of the "Scientific Revolution." But to
suggest that Hooykaas' scholarship is vitiated by apologetic intentions,
as has sometimes been implied, would be a facile and overstated
criticism. His inside knowledge of Calvin's theology was an invaluable
qualification when assessing stronger claims than he made himself for
the relevance of puritan values to the promotion of science. The only
Protestant *doctrine* that he considered germane to that promotion was
the priesthood of all believers, which could encourage a degree of
intellectual liberty. He was sharply critical of scholars who tried to
associate a philosophy of scientific determinism with Calvin's doctrine
of election.[14] A footnote in his discussion of Boyle and natural
theology shows him rebuking those Calvinist theologians who, at the
time of writing, were invoking Calvin himself to justify their Barthian
"No." Hooykaas also kept his distance from Merton's thesis on
puritanism and science,[15] despite obvious affinities between their
views. In one of his contributions to the Open University course
mentioned above, he shrewdly observed that the narrower the definition
of "puritan" the more difficult it was to sustain Merton's thesis, while
the broader the definition the more worthless did the conclusions

---

[14] Hooykaas, *Religion and the Rise of Modern Science* (n. 12), p. 107.

[15] Robert K. Merton, *Science, Technology and Society in Seventeenth-
Century England* (New York: Harper, 1970); originally published in *Osiris* 4
(1938), part 2, 360–632.

become. With reference to the content of scientific knowledge, he had no time for the view that there could be a distinctively Protestant physics, a distinctively Roman Catholic chemistry.[16] Nor did he tolerate the notion that conclusions of scientific worth could ever be deduced from Scripture.[17] The Protestant natural philosophers of the seventeenth century with whom he most sympathized were those, such as Boyle, who did effect a separation—on certain levels at least—between the study of God's two books.

In what respects have more recent writers on science and religion—and on Boyle himself—departed from the style of work that Hooykaas represented? Various developments may be noted, some of them bearing out Hooykaas' own insights—if sometimes adapting them in ways that might have surprised him—while others have been at odds with his approach to the subject as a whole. As far as the study of science and religion is concerned, the most typical tendency has been to follow his sensitivity in exploring such matters, indicating the diversity of thought within both Protestant and Catholic cultures. By stressing the varieties of Catholic scientific experience, William B. Ashworth has made it difficult to generalize about the role of Catholic beliefs in the cultivation of the sciences—with the striking conclusion that if one cannot generalize about a Catholic mindset, how much less can one do so for Protestant cultures?[18] In the same collection of essays, Gary Deason shows how far the mechanists of Boyle's generation could be said to depart from Calvin's original prescription of divine sovereignty.[19] It has also been suggested that attitudes towards a challenging scientific innovation such as the Copernican system were shaped more by the dialectics between Reformation and Counter-Reformation policies than by principles inherent within either Catholic or Protestant theology[20]: Galileo knew his principle of biblical accommodation as well as any Calvinist. When Hooykaas claimed

---

[16] "The Christian Approach" (n. 3), p. 113.

[17] *Ibidem*, p. 119.

[18] William B. Ashworth, Jr., "Catholicism and Early Modern Science," in *God and Nature: Historical Essays on the Encounter Between Christianity and Science*, ed. David C. Lindberg and Ronald L. Numbers (Berkeley: University of California Press, 1986), 136–66.

[19] Gary B. Deason, "Reformation Theology and the Mechanistic Conception of Nature," in *ibidem*, 167–91.

[20] John Hedley Brooke, *Science and Religion: Some Historical Perspectives* (Cambridge: Cambridge University Press, 1991), 82–116.

that "the biblical view inevitably leads to a rational empiricism which
is fundamentally the modern scientific attitude,"[21] his use of the word
"inevitably" exposed him to a two-pronged critique—that such an
account misses elements in a biblical theology (for example the Fall
narrative) which, in certain contexts, could be obstructive; and secondly
that it minimizes other social and economic preconditions of scientific
research.[22]

Indeed, in recent years historians of scientific methodology have
increasingly drawn on insights from the social sciences,[23] and this has
meant that a different construction has been placed on aspects of the
scientific method of the day—and especially that of Boyle—which
Hooykaas tended to take for granted. In particular, contrary to the
rather simple acceptance of "facts" which characterized Hooykaas and
others of his generation, it proves that the social processes involved in
constituting what could pass muster as an authenticated fact have a
complex and fascinating history of their own. Considerable stress has
thus been laid on the importance of the way in which scientific findings
were produced and legitimated and on the broader overtones of Boyle's
attempt to demarcate the realm of fact from that of hypothesis, while
Boyle's social attitudes have also been seen as powerfully formative of
the scientific norms that he advocated.[24] A further development of this
approach, of more direct relevance to Hooykaas' own concerns, stems
from Peter Dear's adaptation of such ideas in connection with an
observation not dissimilar to one made by Hooykaas himself. In his
section on "Mathematics and Experimental Science," Hooykaas says of
Boyle that his scientific method "is absolutely not suited to draw up *a
priori*, by way of formal mathematical reasoning proceeding from given
axioms, a law as that of free falling bodies." He continues: "Boyle is
too attached to real observation to be able to formulate an ideal law."
A similar insight has been turned by Dear into an ambitious thesis in
which contrasting Catholic and Protestant cultures, principally through
their different attitudes towards the miraculous, are said to have
produced contrasting styles of science—the Catholic mechanists

---

[21] "The Christian Approach" (n. 3), p. 124.

[22] Gruner (n. 5).

[23] See, for example, John Schuster and Richard Yeo, eds., *The Politics and
Rhetoric of Scientific Method* (Dordrecht: Reidel, 1986).

[24] Steven Shapin and Simon Schaffer, *Leviathan and the Air-Pump: Hobbes,
Boyle and the Experimental Life* (Princeton: Princeton University Press, 1985);
Shapin, *A Social History of Truth* (Chicago: University of Chicago Press,
1994).

favoring just that formalization of physical laws that Boyle eschewed.[25] If Dear is right, there could, after all, be a distinctively Protestant and a distinctively Catholic physics, the kind of claim that Hooykaas had resisted.

As far as Boyle is concerned, two trends in recent study may be singled out, apart from the reconceptualization of his scientific strategy referred to in the previous paragraph. One is the recognition of the vitality and influence of traditions of thought that it would not have occurred to Hooykaas in the 1940s to take seriously in connection with the Scientific Revolution, namely the role of Paracelsian, Helmontian and alchemical ideas. It now turns out that these were far more central to Boyle's preoccupations than had traditionally been presumed, particularly in his formative years, and this has led to a reconsideration of his matter theory and its relationship to a strict understanding of the mechanical philosophy. As Antonio Clericuzio has put it, "Boyle's chemistry was corpuscular, rather than mechanical": in other words, he saw chemistry as a primary way of penetrating nature, and was reluctant to explain chemical phenomena by having recourse to the mechanical properties of particles.[26] Linked to this was a fascination by alchemy which is again at odds with the traditional image of Boyle as rejecting alchemical traditions and thus founding the modern science of chemistry: this concern on Boyle's part spanned his career from his collaboration with the American alchemist, George Starkey, in the early 1650s, to his last years, and its full implications have yet to be worked out.[27] Revaluation of these facets in Boyle's ideas necessitates the reconsideration, not only of certain of Hooykaas' presuppositions, but

---

[25] Peter Dear, "Miracles, Experiments, and the Ordinary Course of Nature," *Isis* 81 (1990): 663–83.

[26] Antonio Clericuzio, "A Redefinition of Boyle's Chemistry and Corpuscular Philosophy," *Annals of Science* 47 (1990): 561–89. See also his "From Van Helmont to Boyle: A Study of the Transmission of Helmontian Chemical and Medical Theories in Seventeenth-Century England," *British Journal for the History of Science* 26 (1993): 303–34.

[27] See Lawrence Principe, "Boyle's Alchemical Pursuits," and William Newman, "Boyle's Debt to Corpuscular Alchemy," in Michael Hunter, ed., *Robert Boyle Reconsidered* (Cambridge: Cambridge University Press, 1994), 91–118. See also Michael Hunter, "Alchemy, Magic and Moralism in the Thought of Robert Boyle," *British Journal for the History of Science* 23 (1990): 387–410; Lawrence Principe, "Robert Boyle's Alchemical Secrecy: Codes, Ciphers and Concealments," *Ambix* 39 (1992): 63–74; William Newman, *Gehennical Fire: The Lives of George Starkey, an American Alchemist in the Scientific Revolution* (Cambridge, Mass.: Harvard University Press, 1994).

also of those of the generation of Boyle scholars who followed him in
the 1950s, perhaps particularly the influential work of Marie Boas
Hall.[28] Indeed, insofar as their work was more specifically focused on
such issues, this revision has affected their findings more than it has
Hooykaas' own.

Such fresh thought about Boyle's scientific ideas has been based at
least in part on material surviving among Boyle's unpublished papers,
and perhaps the most important development in our understanding of
Boyle since Hooykaas' time has been the tabulation and exploitation of
his extensive manuscripts, of the existence of which Hooykaas appears
not to have been aware. In fact, the Royal Society has since 1769
possessed a deposit comprising a large collection of letters now bound
up in seven guardbooks, together with nearly seventy volumes of
disparate manuscript material which importantly supplement the printed
works collected by Thomas Birch in the eighteenth century and on
which Hooykaas was dependent.[29] The most important implication of
intensive study of this material has been to make it possible to present
a more evolutionary view of Boyle's intellectual activity, starting with
a pre-scientific phase in the 1640s, when he compiled essays on moral
and spiritual edification, and developing through his contact with the
group of natural philosophers which convened at Oxford in the 1650s
to the mature treatises that he wrote in the last thirty years of his
life.[30] Stress is thus laid on the element of change in Boyle's

---

[28] Marie Boas [Hall], "The Establishment of the Mechanical Philosophy,"
Osiris 10 (1952): 412–541; idem, *Robert Boyle and Seventeenth-Century
Chemistry* (Cambridge: Cambridge University Press, 1958). See also T. S.
Kuhn, "Robert Boyle and Structural Chemistry in the Seventeenth Century,"
Isis 43 (1952): 12–36.

[29] See Michael Hunter, *Letters and Papers of Robert Boyle: A Guide to the
Manuscripts and Microfilm* (Bethesda, Md.: University Publications of
America, 1992). For ancillary studies see the works of R. E. W. Maddison
listed in the bibliography to Hunter, *Robert Boyle Reconsidered*.

[30] See esp. Michael Hunter, "How Boyle Became a Scientist," *History of
Science* 33 (1995): 59–103; Lawrence Principe, "Virtuous Romance and
Ingenious Virtuoso: The Shaping of Robert Boyle's Literary Style," *Journal of
the History of Ideas* 56 (1995): 377–97. On Boyle's links with the Oxford
group, see the important study of R. G. Frank, *Harvey and the Oxford
Physiologists: A Study of Scientific Ideas and Social Interaction* (Berkeley and
Los Angeles: University of California Press, 1980). For Boyle's early writings,
see John T. Harwood, ed., *The Early Essays and Ethics of Robert Boyle*
(Carbondale and Edwardsville: Southern Illinois University Press, 1991). The
first to exploit these was J. R. Jacob, *Robert Boyle and the English Revolution*

intellectual concerns during the course of his long career as a natural philosopher. Hooykaas was not wholly unaware of this, occasionally commenting on the appearance of ideas in what he described as "Boyle's earliest works" (by which he meant works published in the early 1660s). In general, however, he tended to treat Boyle's thought as a static system. This trait—shared by many commentators on Boyle even today—was encouraged by Birch's edition, on which Hooykaas seems almost exclusively to have relied, which, though presenting Boyle's works mostly in order of publication, failed to give their dates.

Such an evolutionary view also has an effect on the treatment of Boyle's preoccupations in specific works, encouraging more attention to the contemporary debates which particularly concerned him at different moments in his life.[31] Moreover, in reconstructing the context to which Boyle thus responded, it would be surprising if fifty years of study had not altered our view, not only of Boyle's intellectual milieu, but also of his religious and political setting. Hooykaas' view of this is not unperceptive, due in part to his characteristic reliance, not on the secondary sources of his day, but on such primary sources as Pepys' diary. But his view of the state of religion and politics in the Interregnum and Restoration period is at times rather caricatured, and may usefully be supplemented by the more nuanced and sympathetic view to be found in modern scholarship.[32] This in turn affects our view of Boyle's role in relation to the doctrinal debates of his day, while exploitation of manuscript material relating to Boyle has also led to a fresh understanding of his own intense religiosity, revealing the pessimism about the potential for penetrating this (expressed by

---

(New York: Burtt Franklin, 1977); subsequently, use has been made of them in Malcolm Oster, "'The Beame of Divinity': Animal Suffering in the Early Thought of Robert Boyle," *British Journal for the History of Science* 22 (1989): 151–79, and "Biography, Culture and Science: The Formative Years of Robert Boyle," *History of Science* 31 (1993): 177–226.

[31] See, for instance, Jan Wojcik, "The Theological Context of Boyle's *Things Above Reason*," in Hunter, *Robert Boyle Reconsidered*, 139–55; Michael Hunter and Edward B. Davis, "The Making of Robert Boyle's *Free Enquiry into the Vulgarly Receiv'd Notion of Nature* (1686)," *Early Science and Medicine* (in press).

[32] See, for instance, John Spurr, *The Restoration Church of England, 1646–89* (New Haven: Yale University Press, 1991). For an example of more detailed work relevant to Hooykaas' concerns, see Richard Ashcraft, "Latitudinarianism and Toleration: Historical Myth versus Political History," in *Philosophy, Science and Religion in England, 1640-1700*, ed. Richard Kroll et al. (Cambridge: Cambridge University Press, 1992), 151–77.

Hooykaas in his section on "The Nature of Boyle's Faith") as to some extent premature. Indeed, paradoxically, Boyle proves to bear out to a greater extent than Hooykaas evidently expected the link between the pursuit of science and the heightened religiosity of the Reformation era which he himself stressed in other writings.[33]

Similarly with other aspects of Boyle's thought, on which, during the past few decades, there have been more detailed studies of many of the themes that Hooykaas explored. Any who read his study will wish to supplement it by recourse to such more recent findings. Examples of these include Rose-Mary Sargent's recent detailed account of Boyle's philosophy of experiment;[34] Alan Chalmers' exploration of the complications in Boyle's adherence to the mechanical philosophy;[35] Margaret Osler's account of Boyle's debt to Gassendi;[36] J.E. McGuire's penetrating study of Boyle's voluntarist conception of nature;[37] the attention of Rosalie Colie and R.M. Burns to his views on miracles;[38] the studies of Timothy Shanahan and Edward B. Davis

---

[33] See Michael Hunter, "The Conscience of Robert Boyle: Functionalism, 'Dysfunctionalism' and the Task of Historical Understanding," in *Renaissance and Revolution*, ed. J. V. Field and F. A. J. L. James (Cambridge: Cambridge University Press, 1993): 147–59; idem, *Robert Boyle by Himself and His Friends* (London: Pickering and Chatto, 1994), esp. lxiiif.

[34] Rose-Mary Sargent, *The Diffident Naturalist: Robert Boyle and the Philosophy of Experiment* (Chicago: University of Chicago Press, 1995).

[35] Alan Chalmers, "The Lack of Excellency of Boyle's Mechanical Philosophy," *Studies in the History and Philosophy of Science* 24 (1993): 541–64.

[36] Margaret Osler, "The Intellectual Sources of Boyle's Philosophy of Nature: Gassendi's Voluntarism and Boyle's Physico-Theological Project," in *Philosophy, Science and Religion in England* (note 32), 178–98; see also her *Divine Will and the Mechanical Philosophy* (Cambridge: Cambridge University Press, 1994).

[37] J. E. McGuire, "Boyle's Conception of Nature," *Journal of the History of Ideas* 33 (1972): 523–42. See also Timothy Shanahan, "God and Nature in the Thought of Robert Boyle," *Journal of the History of Philosophy* 26 (1988): 547–66.

[38] R. L. Colie, "Spinoza in England, 1665–1730," *Proceedings of the American Philosophical Society* 107 (1963): 189–213; R. M. Burns, *The Great Debate on Miracles; from Joseph Glanvill to David Hume* (Lewisburg: Bucknell University Press, 1981). See also R. S. Westfall, *Science and Religion in Seventeenth-Century England* (New Haven: Yale University Press, 1958).

of his views on Descartes and final causes;[39] and Jan Wojcik's work—published and forthcoming—on his opinions concerning Things above Reason.[40] The list could be extended, and in each case, there is much to add to what Hooykaas said in this book. Yet, due not least to the extent to which his views were anchored in his study of Boyle's own writings, Hooykaas' succinct remarks often remain almost uncannily perceptive. Indeed, although the trend in recent study has been to emphasize the evolutionary and contingent element of Boyle's thought, a place clearly remains for the exposition of its broader principles. It is this which Hooykaas provides, arguably with more success than others who have attempted similar accounts, partly due to the sophistication on Hooykaas' part which has already been sketched.[41]

Hence, both for what it tells us about Hooykaas himself and what it reveals about Boyle, this work is richly deserving of the new lease of life which its publication in English will give it. Students of Boyle will benefit from Hooykaas' insights into Boyle's ideas, while those interested in Hooykaas himself will at last be able to see the *magnum opus* which wartime circumstances so long conspired virtually to bury from sight.

JOHN HEDLEY BROOKE
Department of History
Lancaster University

MICHAEL HUNTER
Department of History
Birkbeck College
University of London

---

[39] Edward B. Davis, "Parcere nominibus: Boyle, Hooke and the Rhetorical Interpretation of Descartes," and Timothy Shanahan, "Teleological Reasoning in Boyle's *Disquisition About Final Causes*," both in Hunter, *Robert Boyle Reconsidered*, 157–92.

[40] See Wojcik, "Theological Context" (n. 31).

[41] For instance, M. S. Fisher, *Robert Boyle: Devout Naturalist* (Philadelphia: Oshiver Studio Press, 1945); R. M. Hunt, *The Place of Religion in the Science of Robert Boyle* (Pittsburgh: University of Pittsburgh Press, 1955); E. M. Klaaren, *Religious Origins of Modern Science: Belief in Creation in Seventeenth-Century Thought* (Grand Rapids, Mich.: William B. Eerdmans, 1977).

INTRODUCTION

Robert Boyle (1626-91) is generally known for Boyle's Law, which states that for a given amount of gas the product of its volume and pressure is constant. This law has only a minor place, however, in one of his least important works. Boyle is also known as one of the founders of modern chemistry and as a champion of the mechanistic conception of nature. It has been all but forgotten that he takes his place among the eminent apologists of the Christian religion. These levels of reputation are in reverse order of what he himself intended and expected. He engaged in chemistry because it provided material for natural philosophy, and natural philosophy for him stood entirely in the service of religion. Boyle considered his highest task in life to be the glorification of the Creator through knowledge of His creation.

It is regrettable that his apologetic works have been largely forgotten, even among fellow Christians.[1] The defenders of the Christian religion in the 18th and 19th century were almost all laymen in the field of science; they were often naive and timid with respect to this daunting force; they snatched eagerly at the argument that prominent scientists too had been believers.

Boyle held a much stronger position, however, since he was himself one of the foremost promoters of the mechanistic philosophy and yet did not restrict his religion to religious observances. He was not afraid of determinism, being to some degree an adherent of it himself; he wielded a choice of arguments that would have challenged even a nineteenth-century materialist.

---

[1] It was the late Dr. Ch. M. van Deventer, himself an admirer of Boyle, who in 1930 encouraged me to undertake the present study.

Boyle's physico-theological works contain the first broad exposition of the relation between the young "modern" science and religion; they are the first to set Christian belief against the deterministic world-picture that had arisen since Gassendi and Descartes.[1] His expositions are more original and fresh than those advanced in the avalanche of teleological literature unleashed in the 18th century following Newton, a literature that inclines much more towards deism and is influenced already by Locke. But despite the fact that his work exerted a powerful influence in the 17th century and that he led the parade of apologetic writings based on natural philosophy, Boyle became a neglected figure because the fame of his younger contemporary Newton overshadowed everything.[2]

Much has been written about Boyle's contributions to chemistry,[3] though seldom on the basis of a proper study of the original sources or within the context of the science of his day. Boyle's corpuscular philosophy has been the object of repeated study, but accounts with explanatory details have been more prominent than careful comparisons with contemporaries or analysis of his epistemological standpoint.[4] His theology, however, has fared even worse, while a comprehensive and coherent study of Boyle's thought against the backdrop of his time is lacking altogether.

The present essay is an attempt to fill this gap somewhat. I have not tried in the first place to describe in detail Boyle's scientific experiments and his explanations of them in terms of the corpuscular theory. Nor do I pay much attention to his refutations of the errors of chemists and scholastics. My aim has been, rather, to discuss those things that are essential for a full characterization. I wish to give an analysis of his scientific method and his epistemological standpoint, of his attitude

---

[1] Not since Newton, as is sometimes mistakenly asserted; see next note.

[2] F. A. Lange, *Geschichte des Materialismus* (1866; 2d ed., 1875), vol. I, writes correctly: "Posterity sees these two men separated by a big gulf. Boyle is mentioned only in the history of chemistry and his significance for modern culture is almost forgotten, while the name Newton shines like a star of the first magnitude. Their contemporaries did not see things in quite the same way and even less may critical historical research persist in these assessments." It was due to his mathematical genius, we think, that Newton towered above Boyle and became indeed of greater significance for science.

[3] The best is Ch. M. van Deventer, *Schetsen uit de geschiedenis der scheikunde* (Amsterdam, 1884); idem, *Grepen uit de geschiedenis der chemie* (Haarlem, 1924), pp. 197ff.

[4] See esp. Kurd Lasswitz, *Geschichte der Atomistik vom Mittelalter bis Newton* (Leipzig, 1889), 2:261ff.

toward Experience and Reason. Next, I want to offer a similar analysis of his conception of Religion and the role it assigns to Reason and Experience, as well as a critical investigation of his standpoint with respect to natural and revealed religion and his apologetic method. Finally, I hope to show that his scientific and his religious works are ruled throughout by the same spirit.

Completeness could not be my aim; the limits imposed upon this study did not allow me to trace in detail how far his views in science and religion were influenced by others (and who these others were). There is no question that much of it was common property in his circles. I did not get so far as to investigate his influence on younger contemporaries, either in science or in apologetics.

Nevertheless it is my hope that this essay signals the start of a wider study of this great scientist and makes a contribution to our knowledge of science and religion in the 17th century, a century that was decisive for the development of modern thought and that wrestled with problems which to a large extent are still with us.[1]

NOTE TO THE ENGLISH EDITION

This small book was written in 1943 when the German occupation authorities threatened to dissolve the Christelijke Vereeniging van Natuur- en Geneeskundigen in Nederland. The Society wanted to spend the balance of its liquid assets on a final, somewhat larger issue of its quarterly, the *Orgaan*. The offprint bore no year of publication: it was more or less clandestine as no approbation had been applied for at the "Kulturkammer" in The Hague; for that matter, an article in a *periodical* still needed no imprimatur. The work was written under exceedingly difficult circumstances: the Nazi terror (house searches, threats, etc.) was intensifying; nor was it easy to consult library books. The present translation from the Dutch was prepared by Prof. H. Van

---

[1] I wish to thank the editors of this journal for the accommodating way in which they facilitated publication of this essay, in particular Professor G. J. Sizoo, whose interest in the subject helped me decide to finish it.

Dyke for the Pascal Centre for Advanced Studies in Faith and Science, a division of Redeemer College, Ancaster, Ontario.

R. H.
Zeist, The Netherlands
Spring, 1991

TRANSLATOR'S NOTE

As he handed me his personal copy of *Robert Boyle, een Studie over Natuurwetenschap en Christendom*, during a visit at his home on 3 May 1991, Professor Hooykaas remarked that he was still pleased with this early essay of his, though here and there he had indicated a change of mind about a particular interpretation. Also, as he had originally used the first edition of Boyle's *Works* while the second edition is now much more widely available, he had made a beginning of locating and recording the equivalent citations in the second edition and expressed his wish that this be carried through consistently for the English edition. Once home, I completed this task with the able assistance of Lara Schat. How impressive, the thoroughness with which Hooykaas had canvassed his source to take the measure of the mind of Boyle! For ease of reading, some spellings and punctuations in direct quotations from Boyle have been slightly modernized. Hooykaas' copy of his book, showing small deletions and stylistic changes along with pencilled comments in the margin, now rests in the archives of the Pascal Centre. Special thanks go to Marina van der Meer for proofreading, editing, indexing and preparation of the manuscript for publication. This translation was supported in part by a grant from the Social Sciences and Humanities Council of Canada to the Pascal Centre, Redeemer College in Ancaster, Ontario.

H. V. D.

Chapter I

BOYLE'S LIFE AND TIMES

§ 1. Religious Life

Religious life in England, like its art and science, differs markedly from that on the Continent. The Reformation had its own forerunners here, such as John Wycliffe, and was also strongly influenced by John Calvin. At its deepest level it arose from the religious consciousness of the people.

Another, quite different cause of the English Reformation was the pursuit of an autonomous English church, independent of Rome, the movement for Anglicanism that emerged from the rivalry between king and pope rather than from a desire for a purified church. It was not to be expected that these two currents could in the end be channelled into a single movement. The reformers too got into conflict with the king and although under Edward VII the Calvinist confession triumphed in the state church, this did not mean that a lasting unity was achieved. Next to the episcopalians we find the presbyterians, who were Calvinist also with respect to polity, and alongside these two arose the independents, who pushed Protestant liberty to its extremes. We must not think, however, that there were three churches with episcopalian, presbyterian and congregationalist governments. Rather, the shades of opinion were innumerable; moreover, to work for a particular polity did not always mean that one had broken with the established church.

In Cromwell's days the established church was Puritan. Following the restoration of the Stuarts many of the clergy "conformed": they simply put their surplices back on and resumed the old liturgy without necessarily changing their beliefs.[1]

---

[1] *Diary* of Samuel Pepys, 5 Oct. 1662; 26 Oct. 1662.

Thinking of Henry VIII, Edward VII, Bloody Mary, Elizabeth, James I and Charles I, we are at once reminded of the great changes in ecclesiastical policy that were imposed from above in the space of a hundred years. After Charles I was deposed we first see the triumph of the presbyterians, and then of the "fanatick" independents under Oliver Cromwell, while after the abdication of Richard Cromwell, in 1660, a presbyterian parliament restored Charles II to the throne.

By that date, the decades of religious and political controversy, as well as the persecutions that broke out each time a new party came to power, had instilled in many a growing indifference if not aversion toward the deeper questions of life. People longed only for peace and unity. In reaction to the political confusion, absolute monarchy was glorified by the school of Hobbes; in reaction to the austere public morality of the Commonwealth, people turned to the pleasures of life and mocked all moral codes as Puritan hypocrisy[1]; in reaction to the religious disunity there was a move toward unity in the established episcopal church, albeit more in the official institution than in its confession.

A surface morality, a superficial science, a shallow religion—these became, not the starting-point but the cloak for a libertine and sceptical posture in life.[2] The Commonwealth was followed by the "merry

---

[1] Theatre especially, which was rehabilitated under Charles II and now also admitted women to the stage, became a hotbed of immorality. In 1669, Dr. John Wallis writes to Boyle that the play produced at the opening of the Sheldonian in Oxford gave "general offence to all honest spectators" yet was not interrupted by the authorities present even though it was "abominably scurrilous." *The Works of the Honourable Robert Boyle* (2d ed.; London, 1772); *Letters*; 6:459. (Boyle's *Works* are hereafter cited by the title of the individual piece, followed by volume and page number.)

Macaulay, *History of England* (ed. Tauchner, 1849), vol. I, writes: "From the day on which the theatres were reopened they became seminaries of vice" (p. 395); "The war between wit and Puritanism soon became a war between wit and morality" (p. 399; see also p. 177).

[2] This came to expression in obscene and blasphemous language. John Wallis writes to Boyle that at the dedication of the new facility the university had written to the archbishop a letter so profane (it addressed him as "our creator and redeemer") that he (Wallis) had not been able to sign his name to it. Wallis to Boyle, 17 July 1669; *Letters*; 6:459. If this was being done by the spiritual leaders, the nobility was in an even worse condition. Pepys, who became increasingly irritated at the religious scepticism of his patron, Lord Sandwich, once happened upon him while composing an anthem all the while uttering a stream of profanities, "a new custom" (*Diary*, 14 Dec. 1663). To combat this

reign. " Samuel Pepys recounts in his diary that Charles II upon landing in Dover accepted the gift of a Bible and remarked very piously that this was what he "loved above all things in the world."[1] But his reading of it appears to have borne little fruit, for a year later the English court had become notorious for its loose morals and religious indifference. The direction of ecclesiastical policy was determined by the interests of the king and—the Stuarts of the Restoration, too, had learned nothing—the bishops took revenge on the nonconformists in the name of the king and were a match for their royal master in worldliness and ostentation.[2]

There was also, however, another, more dignified reaction to the religious intolerance and dissension of the preceding period, one that was at the same time a reaction to the new intolerance and the frivolity of the Stuart reign. A broad circle of prominent men tried to effect a synthesis by highlighting the cardinal points on which all Christians agreed and by emphasizing Christian morality which threatened to be forgotten in the welter of theology and politics. Their effort was to moderate religious passion by the deliberations of a cool mind. At the same time they resisted atheists and deists, who in those days often invoked reason and science to cover a dissolute lifestyle. Hobbes in particular was their black sheep; he defended a form of caesaropapism that was completely indifferent to the intrinsic truth of Christianity.[3]

---

widespread sin, Boyle wrote *A Free Discourse Against Customary Swearing, and a Dissuasive From Cursing* (6:1-27).

Macaulay writes that as the Puritans never opened their mouths "except in scriptural phrase, the new breed of wits and fine gentlemen never opened their mouths without uttering ribaldry of which a porter would now be ashamed, and without calling on their Maker to curse them . . . and damn them." *History of England*, 1:393.

[1] *Diary*, 25 May 1660. Soon it became evident, however, that his mistress, Lady Castlemaine, won out; even the navy credits in part ended up in her pockets! (*Diary*, 10 Oct. 1666; 12 Dec. 1666.) Charles' popularity quickly came to an end. (*Diary*, 19 Oct. 1662; 30 Nov. 1662; 31 Dec. 1662.) "A sad, vicious, negligent Court [is making] all sober men there fearful of the ruin of the whole kingdom this next year," writes Pepys, who was not exactly a paragon of virtue himself! (*Diary*, 31 Dec. 1666.)

[2] Macaulay, *History of England*, 1:174-76.

[3] Macaulay writes: "Ethical philosophy had recently taken a form well suited to please a generation equally devoted to monarchy and to vice. Thomas Hobbes had maintained . . . that the will of the prince was the standard for right and wrong, and that every subject ought to be ready to profess Popery, Mahometanism, or Paganism at the royal command. Thousands who were

They looked for a middle ground between an exaggerated traditionalism and revolutionary licentiousness, between worldliness and religious fanaticism, between Anglican formality and Puritan formlessness. Their mode of thought was matter-of-fact, intellectual, scientific and balanced. Animated neither by conservatism nor by revolutionary zeal, they were moderately orthodox, middle class and liberal in outlook. They were for the greater part episcopalians, but who bore no ill will

---

incompetent to appreciate what was really valuable in his speculations, eagerly welcomed a theory which, while it exalted the kingly office, relaxed the obligations of morality, and degraded religion into a mere affair of state. Hobbism soon became an almost essential part of the character of the fine gentleman." *History of England*, 1:177; see also Boyle, *Against Hobbes*; 1:187.

"The restored Church contended indeed against the prevailing immorality, but contended feebly, and with half a heart. . . . Her attention was elsewhere engaged. Her whole soul was in the work of crushing the Puritans, and of teaching her disciples to give unto Caesar the things which were Caesar's. . . . Thus the clergy made war on schism with so much vigour that they had little leisure to make war on vice." Macaulay, *History of England*, 1:178.

From Pepys' *Diary*, too, it emerges over and over again that this complaint against the Restoration church was justified. The opposite can be said of the Low Church group, which had little influence for the time being; they declaimed against the loose morals and desired to win the dissenters by being conciliatory.

The extent to which Boyle's circles regarded loose morals, a superficial High Church party, and contempt for experimental science as a single combination, with Hobbes as their philosophical spokesman, is evident from a letter by John Beale: "[A]ll true-hearted Englishmen are aggrieved to see the swarms and prevalence of Hobbians, . . . atheists and scoffers, theatrical buffoons, blasphemers, and the burlesque and travesty which explode all religion, graces and virtues. . . . [T]hese have done more real damages and dishonour to the king, and to our nation, than all the dissenters in their several disguises have been hitherto able to do. And they seem to me more dangerous than all our bloody wars with foreigners, the great plague, and the firing of London." Beale to Boyle, 26 June 1682; *Letters*; 6:445.

The extent to which the opponents in turn regarded the new philosophy, the dissenters, and 'comprehension' as being all of a piece is plain from the oration delivered by Dr. South in Oxford, "the first part of which consisted of satyrical invectives against Cromwell, fanatics, the Royal Society, and new philosophy; the next, of encomiastics in praise of the archbishop, the theatre, the vice-chancellor, the architect, and the painter; the last, of execrations against fanatics, conventicles, comprehension and new philosophy, damning them *ad inferos, ad gehennam*." Wallis to Boyle, 17 July 1669; *Letters*; 6:459. In plain English, the groups thus lumped together were all alike consigned to hell!

toward the nonconformists since they regarded polity, in fact the very confessions, as relative. Later, when under James II the menace of "Popery" united all Protestants and brought William III to the throne,[1] it appeared as if their ideals would triumph. Comprehension and the Edict of Toleration were fruits of their efforts. Against the reaction, the "revolution" of 1689 restored the spirit of 1640, now guided into more peaceful channels. Many of these men were given a bishop's see by William III: Burnet became bishop of Salisbury (1689); Tillotson became archbishop of Canterbury (1691). The name "latitudinarian" dates from this time, for these men tried to exercise the broadest latitude possible in embracing ("comprehending") everybody in the Established Church. That their adaptability in the end repelled men of principle was to be expected. In this way the group that wanted to unite everyone became itself a party, but a party that put a permanent stamp on English religious life.

§ 2. Deists and Apologists

The period of the Restoration brought not only moral dissolution but also a movement to dissolve all ties with the Christian religion. This came to expression in the atheism that blew over from France, and in the typically English school of deism.[2]

Deism is customarily defined as the doctrine that God gave the world its laws and then left it to its fate: God fashioned the clockwork (perhaps also the material of which it is made, although the aristotelian deists deny this), he wound it up, and then he let it run on its own. This description holds only for a special group of deists; there were also plenty of deists who acknowledged God's constant concern with creation. For that matter, the clockwork image is not characteristic of deists alone; their opponents too—the Christian apologists of the 17th

---

[1] The English, curiously, refer to this relatively quiet change, which once for all guaranteed a constitutional monarchy, as a "glorious revolution", while Cromwell's reign, as going too far, is called a "usurpation."

[2] Lord Herbert of Cherbury is regarded as the first deistic writer, but the flowering of English deism did not commence until after Boyle's death, in the first half of the eighteenth century, with such men as Toland and Tindal. Cf. G. V. Lechler, *Geschichte des englischen Deismus* (Stuttgart, 1841). Atheism revived in Italy, from there it spread to France (the seventeenth-century scientist Mersenne estimated the number of atheists and deists at 60,000), and finally blew over to England. In 1681 Tillotson writes that in the last century atheism has travelled over the Alps, infected France, and of late has crossed the Channel and invaded our nation. *Letters*; 6:448.

century, including Boyle—use it repeatedly in combating atheism. They see in the strict regularity and functionality of the machinery of nature a proof of an almighty Creator and Providence. A much more defining characteristic of deists is their neglect of revealed religion. They argue that the natural light is sufficient to arrive at pure religion and this light is the same among pagans and Christians.[1]

Bearing a remarkable affinity with them in many respects are the Christian apologists, who almost always emerge from among the latitudinarians. To be sure, unlike the deists they do accept the Christian revelation as laid down in Holy Scripture, but they would not do this if natural reason did not assent to it. However, reason acknowledges the truth of revelation only afterwards, since it is incapable of discovering by its own powers the mysteries concealed therein. Thus both deists and apologists are convinced of the excellency of reason; both believe their case must be fought with rational arguments; both recognize the legitimate role of natural theology and defend it against atheism in such a fashion that we can sometimes no longer tell whether we are reading deist or orthodox writers. No wonder that many of the arguments used by the defenders of a rational Christian religion later turned out to be useful to their opponents.

The rationalism of the apologists stands in sharp contrast with the authoritarian belief of the Romanizers and the experiential emphasis of the sectaries. The apologists eschewed all extremism; their "rationality" was especially bent on deriving moral precepts from Scripture. Doctrines like that of the Trinity they pushed to the background, even though they did not deny them; a strict doctrine of predestination, from their moderate viewpoint, would lead to dangerous conclusions. It is understandable, therefore, that they were accused of unitarianism and socinianism; in any event, they were not far removed from the Arminian standpoint.

From 1640-1660 the established church had been completely under the influence of Puritanism. There is no question that this continued to have its effect on the latitudinarians. Like all true Protestants they recognized, with the Puritans, Holy Scripture as the only authoritative revelation. In their circles, however, the confessions receded to the background, as did those dogmas that were not all that clearly expressed in Scripture. Puritanism, with its independentist

---

[1] The use of the term "theism" in the modern sense, as opposed to deism and atheism, dates from later times. Boyle uses the labels "theism" and "deism" interchangeably for those who acknowledge only "natural religion" or regard it as sufficient. What we today call "deism" comprises only a fraction of it.

polity, was able to contribute very little to the formulation of confessions. It left the interpretation of Scripture largely to the individual and
was therefore vulnerable to fragmentation. The apologists, by contrast,
were confident that a sober, scholarly inquiry into the Bible would lead
to identical results among all reasonable people and that if there were
any differences these would be so small as not to warrant a break with
the official church. Thus they differed from the independentist Puritans
in that they were not so quick to regard a controversy as a sufficient
cause for separation; their temperament was much more serene and
"rational."

§ 3. Science

In the middle of the 17th century the "new" philosophy celebrated its
triumphs. Now at last, a hundred years after the Reformation,
Scholasticism was severely challenged by Gassendism and Cartesianism. In England this battle was fought in a distinctive way; there
was a tendency not to push the differences to their extremes. Many,
such as Henry More and Ralph Cudworth, adhered to an eclectic
mechanistic philosophy in which Platonic elements were incorporated.
Causal explanation from "efficient" causes, which comes with a
mechanistic view of nature, was usually combined with causal
explanation from final causes which at the same time satisfied religious
sentiments. As a result, with many the opposition between mechanistic
philosophy and theology did not assume the sharp contours we find on
the Continent. There was a moderate scepticism, represented by Joseph
Glanvill, which regarded all systems with some caution without
surrendering itself unconditionally to any one of them.
     English scientists did not simply adopt one of the new philosophi-
cal systems in order to explain the phenomena; they tended rather to
follow in the footsteps of Francis Bacon and pursued an inductive
science by collecting a large body of observed facts. This was then
plausibly "explained" and summarized afterwards with the aid of the
clear and graphic representations of mechanistic philosophy.
     The nerve center of this endeavor was the Royal Society. This
institution had its roots in the Invisible College, a company of learned
men who during the Civil War, in 1645, in order to fight the melan-
choly mood of the time, had begun to devote themselves to the study
of nature and experimental research. Theology and politics were
forbidden subjects. At first the club was based in London, after 1648
partly in London, partly in Oxford. After 1660 it was commuted into
the Royal Society, for Charles II imitated Louis XIV not only in his
vices but also in his patronage of science.

The Royal Society soon had its correspondents all over the world and received from them communications of the most diverse nature: observations of comets, metereological conditions, geological states, and descriptions of indigenous medicine, flora and fauna. This large collection of factual material was meant to contribute to the attainment of a universal "natural history" which Bacon had posited as a necessary condition for the construction of a reliable science. From this arsenal anyone could borrow whatever he needed for drawing up a comprehensive theoretical system. In addition to the collecting of data, deliberate experiments were conducted. The Royal Society adopted a sympathetic attitude toward atomistic and Cartesian philosophy.

The first members of the Royal Society came for a large part from the same circles as the "apologists." The enemies of a tolerant orthodoxy and the enemies of the new philosophy were often the same people: to wit, the reactionaries, centered especially in Oxford, which was High Church and continued to teach medieval peripatetic philosophy; next, Hobbes,[1] who held to his own philosophy and gave offence both religiously and philosophically; finally, the adherents of a "pagan" aristotelian philosophy, who were usually atheists or deists.

The atheists and deists, who appealed to the "new" philosophy, could also best be combated with the new philosophy. Thus England witnessed the curious phenomenon that a moderate orthodoxy defended religion on the basis of experimental science as well as a mechanistic philosophy held in suspicion elsewhere.

§ 4. Robert Boyle (1626–91)

Robert Boyle was the fourteenth child of an Irish nobleman, the Earl of Cork. At a still early age, from 1638 to 1641, he made a journey through France and Italy. His "conversion" dates from that time. A violent thunderstorm confronted him with the question whether he was prepared to die. He made a vow to repent, and Christ, "who had long lain asleep in his conscience," awoke, as he writes himself in a fragment of an autobiography.[2] This was followed, however, by grave doubts about some of the fundamentals of Christianity, which brought him to such a state of depression that only the fact that the Christian religion forbade it kept him from taking his own life. One day, after

---

[1] Macaulay is mistaken, therefore, when he writes that Butler was "the only man of real genius between the Restoration and the Revolution" to show enmity to the new philosophy and the Royal Society (*History of England*, 1:402).

[2] *Life*; 1:xxii.

receiving the sacrament, God restored to him the lost sense of his favor. Since that time he looked upon these impious suggestions "rather as temptations to be suppressed than as doubts to be resolved." Yet he was never thereafter entirely free of these injections, which he called a "disease to my faith." The peculiar advantage of this anxiety was that it brought him to the grounds of his religion, for doubt impelled him to give an account of the fundamentals of Christianity, the sects, Islam, and Judaism. Although he believed more than he could "comprehend," he did not want to believe more than he could "prove." He did not want to owe the steadfastness of his faith to "ignorance of what might be objected against it." "Though we cannot always give a reason for what we believe, we should be ever able to give a reason why we believe it."[1]

Boyle's observations about his conversion display his serious nature. Religion became the all-ruling force in his life; his science too was made serviceable to it. He did everything to make others share in his happiness. Missions had his warm interest. From 1662 he was a governor of the Corporation for the Propagation of the Gospel in New England. He gave financial support to the translation of the Gospel into Malayan and of Grotius' *De veritate religionis christianae* into Arabic. In England he took up the defence of the Christian faith against those who in the name of reason and science thought they could abandon it, hence against atheists and deists. Especially after 1660 his letters and writings lament "our libertine age," an age in which so many undertake "to deride all that is supernatural, and, whilst they loudly cry up reason, make no better use of it than to employ it, first to depose faith, and then to serve their passions and interests."[2]

In 1647 Boyle visited Holland. Among the famous people he met there was Menasseh Ben Israel, chief rabbi of Amsterdam. Even then he was preoccupied with the "theological use of natural philosophy,"[3] for among the apologists of Christianity Boyle was the man who derived his arguments not from speculation or superficial observation of nature but from painstaking experimental science. It must have been shortly after this that he made a beginning with his chemical studies: at the first mention of chemistry in his letters he complains that his oven arrived "crumbled into as many pieces as we into sects."[4]

---

[1] Ibidem; 1:xxiii.
[2] Ibidem; lxxvii.
[3] Ibidem; xlv.
[4] Ibidem; xxxvi.

The lack of unity in the church saddened him; he wished to let the small differences rest, in order to contend together for the great truths revealed in Scripture. Similarly, Boyle stayed out of the political fray. Among the nonconformists he counted influential friends to whom he remained faithful and some of whom he supported financially[1] even after the Restoration; conversely, during the years of the Commonwealth he gave assistance to royalists. Nevertheless he does not seem to have been sympathetic to the "usurpation,"[2] even though according to his biographer he always spoke with great respect of the government, "even in times which he disliked, and upon occasions which he spared not to condemn."[3] He must have been equally disappointed in the Stuarts, however, especially after they began to promote the romanization.

Experimental research soon brought him into contact with the Invisible College. He attended the meetings in Oxford from 1654 till 1668, when he took up residence in London. Scientific research early gave rise to friendship with the celebrated mathematician and theologian John Wallis, with the astronomer John Ward (afterward bishop of Salisbury), with Christopher Wren, the rebuilder of London after the Great Fire. Among his friends and correspondents we meet scientists like Isaac Newton and Robert Hooke, and physicians like Francis Glisson, Thomas Willis and the anatomist Richard Lower. In 1652 he conducted anatomical research with Sir William Petty in Ireland; later he was a frequent companion of Thomas Sydenham on the doctor's daily round of visits.[4]

Prominent churchmen, too, belonged to his circle of friends. Thomas Barlow, the future bishop of Lincoln, guided his studies of the church fathers. With John Beale, chaplain to Charles II, he kept in

---

[1] *Life*; 1:cxl.

[2] In the days of political confusion prior to the Restoration, Boyle was an advocate of obedience to the lawful ruler through thick and thin, even if he conducts himself unwisely. If supreme authority in the state resides with the strongest, everyone will want to venture a chance to prove himself the strongest, and the right to govern will be claimed by anyone who has the support of money and the army. The weak and poor government of the lawful ruler "may less prejudice the publick than the forward and jarring endeavours of men, that perhaps would be wiser rulers, if they had a right to be so." *Some Occasional Reflections*; 2:414. This pretty well sums up the average opinion of the majority of the people; it hardly shows a high regard for Charles I!

[3] *Life*; 1:cxliii.

[4] Ibidem; liv, lv, lxxxvi.

constant touch about the questions of the day. He joined Edward Stillingfleet, bishop of Worcester, in his campaign against religious persecution. In the last part of his life Gilbert Burnet, the future bishop of Salisbury, was one of his closest friends. In addition, he maintained contact with Richard Baxter, the famous Presbyterian; with John Eliot, missionary among the North American Indians; with Ralph Cudworth, leader of the Cambridge Platonists; with John Wilkins, mathematician and theologian, brother-in-law of Oliver Cromwell who was afterward to become bishop of Chester; and with John Tillotson, the primate of the Church of England under William III.

It is remarkable how intense was the interest in science among many English divines (true also for the 20th century). Many of the clergymen mentioned above were equally theologians and scientists. This can also be said of Boyle. Yet he never wanted to "take holy orders." On more than one occasion after 1660 he declined high ecclesiastical appointment, because by accepting it he would no longer be an unsuspected authority in questions of religion: "it is their trade, they are paid for it" were the arguments by which Boyle says the treatises of the clergy were thrust aside. Another motive for his refusal to join the ranks of the clergy was that he did not feel called to ecclesiastical office by the Holy Spirit.[1]

Boyle reached the high point of his accomplishments in the troubled years around 1660. In 1658 he began his experiments with the vacuum pump; in 1660 appeared his first treatise *Touching the Spring of the Air*; in 1662 followed its *Defence* against Linus (which contains the famous Boyle's Law) as well as that against Hobbes. The year 1661 saw the appearance of what is perhaps his most important work, *The Sceptical Chymist*. His experiments were continually interrupted, however, by the uncertain political situation and the resulting monetary cares, for Boyle had to finance all his research from his own (ample) resources. Later came the Plague, the Great Fire of London, and the unrest caused by the Second Anglo-Dutch War, while at the same time his weakening eyesight posed a chronic hindrance.[2] Owing to all these setbacks his work was sometimes thrown into disarray: time and again he complains that certain manuscripts or instruments have got lost.[3]

---

[1] Ibidem; lx.

[2] Pepys, who likewise suffered from an eye ailment, once turned to Boyle for advice; *Diary*, 22 June 1668.

[3] *Life*; 1:cxxv; cf. 5:583.

For all that, enough has remained to fill five (or six) hefty volumes that make up *The Works of the Honourable Robert Boyle*.[1]

Boyle's style suffers from prolixity. The long-winded titles of his works make one fear the worst for their content. He often needs a whole folio-sized page to inform us that this time he will be brief, and why he will be brief. But though his style is formal, it is also polished; his disquisitions may be tedious, they are also lucid and not without humor. One is struck time and again by pointed sayings and arresting images. His works show that he was exceedingly well read in theology (Roman Catholic and Protestant, Jewish and Islamic), philosophy, science, medicine, philology and travels.[2] He is very conscientious in citing his sources when describing an experiment not first performed by himself or when advancing an idea not original with him. In his scientific polemics he takes great care to be fair to the standpoint of his opponents and to put them in as favorable a light as possible. Though he seems to have been a man of fiery temperament, he exhibits the typical English trait of restraining himself to what is "proper," with the result that his prose at times seems rather prim.

In 1665 appeared *The Experimental History of Cold*, containing important experiments with the thermometer. In 1666 came out the *Origin of Forms and Qualities*, which contains an excellent refutation of the scholastic doctrine of substantial forms. In 1685 was published *A Free Inquiry into the Vulgarly Received Notion of Nature*, whose original arguments unmask the notion of a sovereign "Nature" as an empty concept. This treatise was followed in 1688 by a teleological work, *A Disquisition About the Final Causes of Natural Things*. Finally, in 1690, his main work in apologetics appeared, *The Christian Virtuoso*, which sets forth a definitive statement of the relation between science and religion.

Boyle's private life was uneventful. He had no worries about finances, nor about family matters, since he never married, despite the

---

[1] The first edition came out in 1744 in five volumes folio. The second edition appeared in 1772 in six volumes quarto; it has been made available again in 1965 in a facsimile reprint by Georg Olms Verlag of Hildesheim. All references in the present study are to the second edition.

[2] Because he did not hold public office, he was able to devote all his time to the pursuit of science and learning in the broadest sense. Consequently his intellectual development was broader than that of his more famous contemporaries, including Newton, and this made him especially suitable as an apologist of the Christian religion.

efforts of John Wallis to get him to change his mind.[1] Only his physical health gave him problems; after 1689 it declined rapidly. He died in 1691, shortly after the passing of his sister, Lady Ranelagh, with whom he had lived the latter part of his life.

---

[1] Cf. Wallis to Boyle, 17 July 1669; *Letters*; 6:460; cf. *Life*; 1:cxxxviii.

Chapter II

SCIENCE

§ 1. Experimental Philosophy

For most investigators of nature in the 17th century it went without saying that they should not only describe the facts but also try to determine the place and value of these facts in the total system of human thought. Knowledge of nature was still regarded as experimental philosophy. Consequently, what posterity finds most striking about Boyle is that he was one of the defenders of "mechanical philosophy," thus of a so-called dogmatic philosophical system. This does not alter the fact that he unquestionably put experience above all philosophical speculation. Many before him had already paid lip-service to this, but Boyle put into practice his rule that a good reasoner is dissuaded from the most cogent reasoning by a single experience that contradicts it.[1] Thus he speaks continually of "experimental philosophy."

Boyle regards Francis Bacon as the founder of experimental philosophy. He follows Bacon's maxim, "What nature is or does must not be thought up or reasoned out but discovered."[2] While he respects Gassendi and Descartes, he stands with reverend awe before "that great restorer of physicks, the illustrious Verulam"; "one of the first and greatest experimental philosophers of our age"; "the great architect of experimental history"; "one of the most judicious naturalists that our age can boast."[3]

---

[1] *The Christian Virtuoso;* 5:538.
[2] *The Experimental History of Cold;* 2:462.
[3] *Works;* 2:143; 4:49; 5:511, 514, 528.

Bacon has been reproached for having performed virtually no
deliberate experiments[1] and that when he did perform any at all they
were so inaccurate that one must wonder that the great experimenter
Boyle had such a high regard for him. Boyle even speaks of "our
famous *experimenter*, the Lord Verulam himself."[2] But we must
remember that Boyle himself says that he follows the example of Bacon
in his *Sylva Sylvarum* when he refers to observations and trials alike as
"experiments," since both are "matters of fact" and therefore "historical" in the broad sense.[3] And as for inaccuracy, when Bacon finds the
specific gravity of mercury to be 17 then Boyle imputes this not to
"want of judgment or care" but to a lack of "exact instruments."[4]

According to Boyle, no one more than Bacon saw the necessity of
a natural history, a large collection of observations from nature, and no
one promoted them more than he by precept and example. In a treatise
entitled *Some Considerations Touching Experimental Essays in General*
Boyle now presents a number of simple observations that were
originally intended as a continuation of Bacon's *Sylva Sylvarum; or, A
Natural History.*[5] He expresses the wish that he who is unable to
perform any new experiments should take careful note of phenomena
that can be observed without them, particularly those that support a
familiar truth or that refute a grave error. Attention to these "obvious
phenomena of nature" will provide us with one half of natural history,
the "new experiments" providing the other half.[6] To attain this goal,
Boyle maintained connections with merchants, seafarers and mission-
aries all over the world, who communicated their observations to him.

No more than Bacon, however, does Boyle consider natural
history to be the ultimate goal. He knows that the mind assesses and
orders the facts and cannot help but seek their explanation. Short of
that, science would be nothing but a compilation of isolated data. "An
absolute suspension of the exercise of reasoning were exceeding

---

[1] Justus von Liebig, *Ueber Francis Bacon von Verulam* (Munich, 1863), says
harsh things about him; cf. Kuno Fischer, *Francis Bacon und seine Schule* (3d
ed.; Heidelberg, 1904), p. 335.

[2] *Medicina hydrostatica;* 4:455.

[3] *Experimenta et observationes physicae;* 5:567.

[4] *The Usefulness of Natural Philosophy;* 1:88. That may well be true, but then
Bacon should have taken care to get better instruments, for the Arabs already
had given very accurate specific gravity tables; cf. a table by Al-Biruni (around
A.D. 1000) in *Pogg. Ann. der Physik*, ser. 4, vol. 17 (1859), p. 352.

[5] *Physiological Essays;* 1:306.

[6] Ibidem.

troublesome, if not impossible."[1] The very wish to perform especially
those experiments that support familiar truths or refute grave errors
implies a classification of phenomena. His publication *Experimenta et
observationes physicae* contains a number of isolated experiments, but
also some that belong together by virtue of their purpose or their
subject matter. Following Bacon's example in the *Sylva Sylvarum*,
Boyle calls them "experiments solitary" and "experiments in consort."
Only his "backwardness to frame theories" persuades him "to forbear
as yet to methodize them."[2] The *General History of the Air* (1692) is
a work that deals entirely with a single subject, as does his *Natural
History of Human Blood* (1683) and his *Natural, Experimental History
of Mineral Waters* (1683).[3]

That Boyle does grant reason its proper place comes out most
clearly when he conducts deliberate experiments. For then he consciously eliminates accident or chance and pursues a specific goal, such
as to demonstrate that air has spring, or that there exists a vacuum, or
that the elements of the chemists are compounds.

Boyle's empiricism is a "rational" empiricism. He says that by an
experimental philosopher he does not mean a "vulgar chemist" or a
"mere empirick," who calls only that experimental which makes use
solely of mechanics or chemistry—in short, of mere technical know-
how. Such a person carries out experiments without reflecting upon
them: he is more out to produce effects than to discover truths. No, the
true experimental philosopher or virtuoso gathers observations in order
to reflect upon them and draw profound truths from them.[4]

Thus Boyle keeps his distance from those chemists of his day who
like schoolboys mixed all kinds of substances together in the hope that
somehow gold or medicines would emerge. Although he agrees with
Bacon that science must also seek to be useful to humanity, and
although he himself also looks for practical applications of his
knowledge, nevertheless Boyle's chief aim is "philosophical." It is his
ambition to study chemistry "with a disinterested mind." His design,
said his friend Burnet, "was only to find out nature, to see into what
principles things might be resolved and of what they were compounded,
and to prepare good medicaments for the bodies of men."[5] Boyle
himself testified that he cultivated chemistry "not so much for itself as

---

[1] Ibidem; 303.

[2] *Experimenta et observationes physicae;* 5:167.

[3] See, respectively, 5:609–742; 4:595–644, 745–59; 4:794–821.

[4] *The Christian Virtuoso;* 5:524.

[5] *Life;* 1:cxliv.

for the sake of natural philosophy. " He designed and pursued most of
his experiments "not to multiply processes but to serve for foundations
and other useful materials for an experimental history of nature, on
which a solid theory may in process of time be superstructed. " For this
reason he always selected plain and simple proofs, ones that lend
themselves best for this purpose.[1]

What direction does this theory take? Bacon had not been
successful in moving from "natural history" to an inductive science.
Induction after all was far from being completed and so his attempts
could not but founder. Boyle realizes this and so does not follow Bacon
slavishly. He remarks in 1661 that he had not at the outset read much
of Descartes' *Principia* or Gassendi's *Syntagma* or even Bacon's *Novum
Organum* because he did not want to be "prepossessed with any theory"
before being led by the things themselves in a particular direction.[2]
This direction is that of "mechanical philosophy in general." The
greater part of Boyle's work is not compilational but focuses rather on
experiments designed to confirm the mechanical theory, the corpuscular
theory. Few of his works make mention of any facts without ordering
them in a theoretical framework under the guidance of general
principles. In doing so, the greatest care is exercised with regard to the
theory, and the greatest respect is paid to the facts. He is aware of
making no more than attempts in the direction of the "solid theory"
mentioned above.

Of course, Boyle is not so naive as to mistake observations for the
strictly objective; he knows they are susceptible of error, dependent as
they are on the observer as well as on defective instruments. His
descriptions of experiments—for example, those relating to a
vacuum—are not without a discussion of errors.[3] He remarks that his
own experiments sometimes yield very different results and that
therefore he does not want to construct theories or formulate practical
rules of experience that are based on no more than a single experiment.[4]

§ 2. Chemistry

Boyle's interests in science were many-sided. He was especially
interested in anatomy, particularly because it provided him with the

---

[1] *Life;* 1:cxxx. Cf. *Experimenta et observationes physicae;* 5:598.

[2] *Physiological Essays;* 1:302.

[3] Cf. *Two Essays Concerning the Unsuccessfulness of Experiments;* 1:318–53.

[4] *Physiological Essays;* 1:348f.

most important arguments for his teleological views in natural theology. He was in close contact with Sydenham, Glisson, Willis, Highmore and Lower, important medical practitioners of the time; he was also acquainted with Harvey. But his favorite study was chemistry; he considered it the key of experimental philosophy.[1]

In *The Sceptical Chymist* Boyle demonstrates with many proofs that fire is not the proper means to analyze substances into their components, since in some instances heat does yield the substances of which the compound is composed but in other cases heat modifies the entire texture of the compound with the result that analysis yields other combinations of corpuscles into secondary particles. He shows that in any case neither the four elements of Aristotle nor the three principia of chemists can be regarded as true elements. That Boyle formulated the modern definition of an element, however, is a stubborn misconception.[2] He knows only absolute elements; the analytical concept of element was not introduced until the positivist Lavoisier.[3]

Boyle's merits for chemistry should not be underestimated, even though he has no great discoveries or important laws to his name. But knocking the bottom out of traditional misconceptions by means of experimental proofs is just as much a step in the right direction. Moreover, he certainly did advance practical chemistry, if only by pioneering wet chemistry: precipitate reactions, indicator tests for acids and bases.[4]

Boyle was also of great importance for the development of theoretical chemistry. Because he pursued a "chemical philosophy" on mechanical foundations he emancipated chemistry from the strait-jacket of a theory that had outlived itself. By the first half of the 17th century,

---

[1] *Life*; 1:cxxxi, cxliv, cxlix. *The Producibleness of Chymical Principles;* 1:589, 591.

[2] Found even with a keen historian like Pierre Duhem, *Le mixte et la combinaison chimique* (Paris, 1902), pp. 16f. That this notion is incorrect has been shown by Van Deventer, *Grepen uit de geschiedenis der chemie*, p. 202. See also my doctoral dissertation, *Het Begrip element in zijn historisch-wijsgeerige ontwikkeling* (Utrecht, 1933), pp. 202-4.

[3] See below, p. 55

[4] *Philosophical Transactions* of the Royal Society of London, No. 197; reprinted in Boyle, *Works;* 5:744-50.

knowledge of chemical facts had grown to such an extent that the aristotelian concepts no longer sufficed to express them.[1]

Boyle broke radically with tradition and explained chemical change as a change in the composition and arrangement of corpuscles, an explanation still largely used today. He was acquainted with the concept "secondary particle," not with our concept "molecule," for then he would have had to indicate which substances he wanted to regard as elements.

Yet it is too often ignored that Boyle had important predecessors, such as Sala, Sennert and Jungius.[2] These men had not overcome the old views, however, and as physicians they were too preoccupied with practical objectives. They did not transform chemistry into the auxiliary of general "experimental philosophy."

Boyle is also the first chemist of importance to be at the same time significant for physics; he was the first to practise chemistry consciously as a "science" rather than as an "art." For his goal was knowledge, not in the first place practical utility. Thanks to Boyle, chemistry became, as it were, an official science and emerged from the obscurity of the laboratories into the full light of day. He strongly opposed secrecy and published his findings in language accessible to all. He broke the secrecy surrounding phosphor by publishing the method of preparation he had discovered.[3]

§ 3. Physics

Far more than for his chemical research Boyle is known to us for what is referred to as "Boyle's Law," although he himself would have little

---

[1] Hence those strange combinations of aristotelian and corpuscular notions, the latter especially under the influence of an old medical tradition; see my *Het Begrip element*, pp. 40, 177, 181. See also my "De natuurlijke klassificatie der chemische substanties," *Chemisch Weekblad* 33 (1936): 602ff.

[2] On Sennert, see Kurd Lasswitz, *Geschichte der Atomistik*, 1:436; my *Het Begrip element*, p. 160. On Jungius, see Lasswitz, ibidem, 1:243. On Sala, see my *Het Begrip element*, p. 148.

[3] Cf. Boyle, *A Short Memorial of Some Observations Made Upon an Artificial Substance that Shines Without any Precedent Illustration* (1677); 4:366–70. *The Aerial Noctiluca: Or, Some New Phenomena and a Process of a Factitious Self-Shining Substance* (1680); 4:379–404. *New Experiments and Observations Made Upon the Icy Noctiluca* (1681); 4:469–95.

thought that of all his work this would survive him. This law[1] is hidden in a rather unimportant treatise, *A Defence of the Doctrine Touching the Spring and Weight of the Air Against the Objections of Franciscus Linus* (1662), one of the few polemical treatises of the peace-loving Boyle.[2]

Boyle's Law is therefore linked to his most important investigation in physics, namely into the weight and spring of the air. Since the experiments of Torricelli every scientist on the Continent was engrossed in the problem of a vacuum, and Boyle too was fascinated by it. From a publication of Caspar Schott he learned of the construction of Otto von Guericke's air-pump. This spurred him on to build his own vacuum pump, one that would lend itself better for experiments. In the case of Guericke, a sphere was pumped empty, but one could not insert anything into it. Boyle now invented a "recipient"[3] into which one could introduce objects. Several times he also improved the pump itself so that a better vacuum could be achieved and the operation of the pump made lighter.

For these experiments Robert Hooke (recommended to him by Dr. Willis) was his assistant; Hooke also made the instruments.[4] Boyle investigated the propagation or transmission of sound, light and heat in a vacuum and traced how chemical substances and living beings reacted to a vacuum. He also used a baroscope to gauge the pressure inside the apparatus.[5] With Denis Papin as his assistant he did experiments at low and high pressures; here we encounter for the first time, among other things, an "instrument to distill *in vacuo.*" It was to be a long time, however, before this was included among the conventional procedures of chemistry.[6]

It is an open question to what extent the construction of the instruments was the work of Boyle himself or that of Hooke and Papin.

---

[1] In the 19th century it was customary on the Continent to ascribe the law to Edmé Mariotte (1620–84). Quite wrongly so; Mariotte wrote later and most likely was acquainted with Boyle's work. Euler (1727) and Boerhaave (1732) mention Boyle, not Mariotte.

[2] *Against Linus;* 1:118–85.

[3] The word recipient came into use because a receiving vessel from the chemical art of distillation was used as the container to be pumped empty.

[4] *New Experiments;* 1:7.

[5] *A Continuation of New Experiments;* 3:206, 208.

[6] *The Second Continuation of Physico-Mechanical Experiments;* 4:518.

That they had a hand in it is clear. Boyle, as his biographer says, knew how to pick good assistants.[1]

The *machina Boyleana* became highly popular; a specimen was donated to the Royal Society. The experiments were repeated for the members many times.

Of importance are also Boyle's experiments in the area of thermometry, reported on in his *Experimental History of Cold*.[2] And his *Hydrostatical Paradoxes*[3] is a lucid treatment of hydrostatics with the aid of experiments that are easy to execute, without involving mathematics. These works did not introduce anything that was fundamentally new.

§ 4. Mechanical Philosophy

Compared to Bacon, Boyle pays more attention to "trials" than to ordinary "observations." Unless one works hit or miss, accident plays only a limited role in an experiment. An experiment is the result of a lengthy, prior labor of thought. It is designed for an express purpose; with Boyle the purpose is to find a causal explanation of natural phenomena.

It is here that seventeenth-century rationalism becomes apparent in Boyle. He believes that all things are in principle intelligible. By granting reason a big role in science, however, he does not by that token accept every explanation that professes to be "rational." In scholastic philosophy, too, a rationalistic streak is unmistakable, but in Boyle's opinion scholasticism is not really rational: it uses all kinds of concepts that are incomprehensible, such as occult qualities and substantial forms,[4] and it is better to give no explanation at all than to

---

[1] *Life;* 1:cxliv.

[2] London, 1665; 2:462–734.

[3] Oxford, 1666; 2:738–97.

[4] *The Origin of Forms and Qualities;* 3:13. A recent attempt in A. G. M. van Melsen's doctoral dissertation, *Het Wijsgeerig verleden der atoomtheorie* (Amsterdam, 1941), to "read into" Boyle certain aristotelian notions must be firmly rejected. Van Melsen even goes so far as to say that in Boyle "the idea of an *essential form* is given the *slightly altered* aspect of *structure.*" Structure, however, is an atomistic concept; even if the substantial form is not something that exists apart from the substance, then there still is a world of difference between the aristotelian substantial form and the combination of qualities that results from the structure of a "concretion." Nor will it do to look for influence of the doctrine of minima in Boyle, with Sennert as intermediary. For a *minimum naturale* is perfectly homogeneous; Sennert presupposes "prima

give an unintelligible one.[1] Boyle therefore became a vehement opponent of peripatetic and "chemical" natural philosophies which introduced terms that did not correspond with clear notions.

Boyle contrasts this with mechanical philosophy, which states that the primary principles of explanation are matter and motion, principles which are clear, simple, and intelligible.[2] Motion divides matter into very small particles of different size and form: the *corpuscula*. Thus additional principles of explanation are size, shape, and position of particles. All other qualities can be reduced to these mechanical causes. Nothing is more intelligible or comprehensive, for all sorts of shapes and movements of the particles are possible, hence also all types of texture and all kinds of pores between the material particles.[3] Precisely the "catholicity" of its principles enables mechanical philosophy to incorporate particular physical hypotheses.[4] It can be applied to all natural phenomena that fail of explanation by other principles.[5]

Owing to the clear and unambiguous nature of its principles, mechanical philosophy surpasses the peripatetic and alchemist systems, both of which proceed from obscure and contested principles.[6] The latter resort to non-mechanical causes, with the result that they can explain far less. Motion and change are ascribed to some unmechanical, immaterial principle: world-soul, plastic power, substantial forms, archeus. But *how* these immaterial things cause matter to move remains

---

mista" which are conceived half mechanically, half peripatetically; Boyle presupposes purely mechanical concretions. Does it follow from this that Boyle is therefore influenced by the doctrine of minima? Is it not much more plausible that Sennert was influenced by the corpuscular theory? The claim indeed is often made, though never proved, that Boyle's theory occupies a middle ground between the doctrine of minima and philosophical atomism. Other influences worked on Boyle just as well: not just philosophical schools (in which connection the influence of the medical profession must not be overlooked!) but especially practical experience contributed to the formation of his (and of nearly every other) scientific theory. Our author seems to forget this, as do others who are too engrossed in philosophy. Especially if they subscribe to a particular philosophical system, their zeal causes them to perceive the influence of that system everywhere. [Cf. A. G. van Melsen, *From Atomos to Atoms* (Pittsburgh, 1952), pp. 104-9.]

[1] *Against Linus;* 1:150.
[2] *The Mechanical Hypothesis;* 4:69f.
[3] Ibidem; 70.
[4] Ibidem; 72.
[5] Ibidem; 76.
[6] Ibidem; 69, 76.

shrouded in darkness; one can only say *that* they cause it.[1] Mechanical philosophy, by contrast, sets this clearly before our eyes: motion is transferred from one body to another following mechanical laws. The phenomena of the world are *physically* produced by the "mechanical affections of the parts of matter, and what they operate upon one another according to mechanical laws."[2] For Boyle is convinced that the laws of mechanics hold not only for the large visible bodies but also for the "hidden transactions that pass among the minute particles of bodies."[3]

If a world-soul as mover is to be intelligible and *physical*, says Boyle, it must be reducible to matter and motion. For this reason the *materia subtilis* (subtle matter) of the Cartesians, which is just as active and diffused throughout the universe as the *anima mundi* (world-soul) of the Platonists, is preferable, because it is a subtle *corporeal substance* and operates by virtue of *local motion*.[4]

Because he acknowledges only material causes in science, Boyle has sometimes been viewed as a promoter of the scientific materialism of the 18th and 19th century. He differs from the latter, however, in equally recognizing non-material causes in nature.[5] However, he is absolutely opposed to using them as explanatory means in physics; for Boyle, therefore, materialism is a *method!*

Boyle is also an opponent of the "qualitative" theory of the chemists. They explain the qualities of substances from those of the three principles of Paracelsus: sulphur, mercury and salt, but then the qualities of these principles require an explanation, and that will have to be mechanical and be based upon the peculiar texture of the corpuscles they are composed of.[6]

It is clear from the above citations that Boyle champions the mechanical explanation of nature in general, not any particular form of it. Because the principles of both are "intelligible" he can defend Cartesians and atomists alike against the scholastics. Thus he writes that to explain the expansion of gases, the atomists assume that the corpuscles of a gas

---

[1] *The Mechanical Hypothesis*; 4:71f.

[2] Ibidem; 69.

[3] Ibidem; 71.

[4] Ibidem; 73.

[5] E.g., final causes, which are acknowledged simultaneously with the mechanical causes (not instead of them, every now and then!), and the Final Cause, God. See below, p. 69.

[6] *The Mechanical Hypothesis;* 4:75f.

move away from each other; the Cartesians, that the pores are widened and then filled with aether; the peripatetics, that the same body now completely fills a larger space. If the former explanations perhaps fail to satisfy, Boyle remarks, the latter must be utterly rejected as it is unintelligible. "To explain a thing is to deduce it from something or other in nature more known than itself."[1]

This is not an isolated quotation. Time and again we see Boyle mention Cartesians and atomists in one breath, in opposition to non-mechanical philosophers. Since both parties, he writes, "agree in deducing all the phenomena of nature from matter and local motion, I esteemed that . . . they might be thought to agree in the main, and that their hypotheses might by a person of a reconciling disposition [like Boyle's] be looked on as one philosophy." And since motion plays a large role in mechanical engines, it might be termed the "mechanical hypothesis or philosophy"; again, since it explains things from corpuscles or minute bodies, it may be styled a "corpuscular philosophy."[2] Boyle wants to write for the "Corpuscularians in general," rather than for "any party of them."[3] Thus he is an advocate of "comprehension" not just in theological respects!

§ 5. Rationalism and Empiricism

When Boyle says that he holds all things to be intelligible we should not on that account regard him as a rationalist after the Cartesian model. Next to the power of human reason he also acknowledges, especially on the basis of religious considerations, reason's weakness. For him, all things, at least within the sphere of the physical, are intelligible in principle, but they are not necessarily so in reality. All things are intelligible, but they are not all explicable "by the dim reason of man."[4] There are things that we "might understand well enough if God did make it his work to inform us of them, yet we should never of ourselves find out those truths."[5] Thus for Boyle there can be facts that we do not yet understand, or will never understand, yet which must be acknowledged as true. This is hardly a consistent rationalism. When some of the "modern philosophers" (Cartesians) say that one cannot assent to anything unless one can conceive it clearly, then Boyle

---

[1] *Against Linus;* 1:145.

[2] *Physiological Essays;* 1:356.

[3] *The Origin of Forms and Qualities;* 3:7.

[4] *The Usefulness of Natural Philosophy;* 2:46.

[5] *Things Above Reason;* 4:407.

in principle agrees with them, but he also remarks that a person may, "through partiality or laziness," pretend "that he cannot conceive what he has no mind to assent to." The ancient Epicureans, for example, tell us they cannot frame a notion of an incorporeal substance or spirit, wherefore they reject it.[1] This is a remarkable statement in Boyle: although he accepts the primacy of the understanding over the human will, he is forced to admit here that the will can darken the understanding![2]

Rationalism and empiricism contend for the mastery in Boyle's science, as it does in his philosophy and his religion. Yet in the end, whenever reason and experience clash, experience wins out. His science is an experimental science, however much the reader is struck by his "corpuscular philosophy." It is the experimental nature of his science that imposes limits on reason for him.

The limits to the application of human understanding are the very reason why Boyle the physicist never feels compelled to choose between the competing systems of Descartes and Gassendi and why he never proceeds to erect an alternative system.[3] If he need not choose qua physicist, neither will he choose qua philosopher, for he desires an "experimental philosophy," one in which only that is acknowledged as certain which rests on a solid foundation of facts. Thus he excludes from experimental science whatever is not verifiable and then goes on to show, either that the differences between Gassendists and Cartesians is a metaphysical one, or that no physical decision is as yet possible owing to the incomplete state of experimental science.

Boyle regards the debate about fundamental concepts as a non-physical discourse. He realizes that every definition of fundamental principles ultimately moves in a circle and that we cannot comprehend what, say, "matter" really is. When the philosophical schools pronounce upon it, Boyle will not have physics choose sides: some points of difference between Cartesians and Gassendists (Boyle always calls them "atomists" or "modern Epicureans") "seem to be rather metaphysical than physiological."[4] And therefore he will not decide between Descartes' view that the essence of matter is nothing but extension and Epicurus' view that it is both extension and impenetrability.[5] Because of the uncertainty and polemics about the question whether matter is

---

[1] *The Usefulness of Natural Philosophy;* 2:47.

[2] Cf. below, pp. 60, 66, 83, 84, 92.

[3] Cf. *Physiological Essays;* 1:355.

[4] Ibidem.

[5] *The Possibility of the Resurrection;* 4:198f.

indeterminate or to a certain degree divisible, he refuses to offer explanations in terms of atoms or indivisible corpuscles or in terms of their innate motion.[1] Nor does he want to express a positive opinion on the question whether Epicurus' vacuum or Descartes' "subtle matter" are possible[2]; if one accepts with Descartes that matter and extension coincide, then of course a true vacuum is impossible.[3] From these remarks it is clear that Boyle is no pure atomist; he makes use of minute particles that *approximate* the function of atoms and molecules in modern chemistry.

Beyond the scope of experience, according to Boyle, lie those questions that seem to concern the "explication of the first origin of the universe [rather than of] the state wherein we now find it."[4] As a physicist he wishes to abstain from making a decision about that. The world is "rational," he agrees, but there are perhaps more rational possibilities: we have simply to observe the present fabric of the world and not wonder why precisely these laws of motion obtain rather than others, why precisely "this admirable universe" was established "rather than a world of any other of the numberless constructions God could have given it."[5] Because it cannot be verified through experiment and observation, Boyle dismisses the Cartesian proof that proceeds from the immutability of God[6] and he rejects the view of the ancient atomists that matter is "eternal."

A final limit to the rational in physics is posed by the empirical nature of physical research. That which is not intelligible can yet be true: in that case empirical data cause us to accept it. Yet also, that which is intelligible is not necessarily true: empirical data will determine that. Boyle realizes that everything is related to everything else and that therefore a complete explanation would not be possible until all the phenomena in the world were known. So long as science is not finished we must do with explanations that hold for limited areas only. That being so, more than one rational explanation is sometimes possible, until some of these partial explanations have to be dropped because of the discovery of a new interrelationship. For this reason Boyle will always try to have experimentation decide between two explanations and if that is not successful pin his hopes on the future or

---

[1] *The Origin of Forms and Qualities;* 3:7.
[2] Ibidem.
[3] *Physiological Essays;* 1:355.
[4] Ibidem; 355f.
[5] *The Veneration Owed to God;* 5:149f.
[6] Ibidem; 140.

else present the difference as being of a non-physical nature. In this way rational empirical science triumphs in the physical realm over pure rationalism.[1]

The peculiar struggle in Boyle between his rationalism and his empiricism, and his reluctance to make a clear choice between Descartes and Gassendi, is especially apparent when he deals with the problem of a vacuum. He declares once for all in his *New Experiments Physico-Mechanical Touching the Spring of the Air* that by a vacuum he does not understand a "space wherein there is no body at all," but a space that is either altogether or (given experimental imperfections) almost totally "devoid of air."[2] His experiments with the vacuum pump prove the absence of *air*. Therefore he will not have Hobbes label him and his fellow members of the Royal Society "vacuists"; yet neither does he want to be lumped with the "plenists." He refuses to choose between affirming or denying that an absolute vacuum can exist.[3]

The crass assertion of certain peripatetics that his so-called vacuum contains air is easily refuted by Boyle through experiments. But if one takes vacuum to mean a space perfectly devoid of *all* corporeal substance, then it may be "plausibly enough maintained," says Boyle, that such a thing does not exist.[4] It is impossible that nothing at all is present in Torricelli's space or under the glass receiver of the air-pump, because we can *see* everything in the receiver. That means that light passes through it, and since light arises either from extremely fine corpuscles emanated by the illuminating object (Gassendi), or else from the rapid motion of subtle, aethereal matter (Descartes), therefore there must be *something* there. After all, as the experiment shows, the magnetic effluvia likewise pass through the vacuum.[5]

Although he therefore leaves undecided for the time being which explanation of light to accept, Boyle is convinced that for light (and magnetic force) to be transmitted, matter and motion are required. He wants to be able to comprehend the propagation of light, which becomes incomprehensible if he does not assume a substance that makes it possible.

If his rationalism causes him not to disavow the plenists altogether, his empiricism—his experimental bent—causes him to lean

---

[1] This is true also for the theological domain; see below, pp. 91f, 99, 100f.

[2] *New Experiments;* 1:10.

[3] *Against Hobbes;* 1:191.

[4] *New Experiments;* 1:74.

[5] Ibidem; 32f.

toward the vacuists. He needs the corpuscles of light and magnetism and therefore can hardly accept a complete vacuum of any significant size, a so-called *vacuum coacervatum*, even though he does not explicitly reject it either. On the basis of his own observations, however, he does not consider it certain that the space that is pumped empty is *full* of what he himself calls the "presumed" corpuscles of magnetism and light, since for light to pass through it makes no difference whether air is present or absent and therefore it is not certain that the space left by the air particles after pumping is filled by such corpuscles: it is possible that there is "some aethereal matter" in that space, he writes, but it is not *certain* that this is really so. The plenists (of the Cartesian school) cannot *prove by experiments* that there is something there. They simply postulate that there cannot be a vacuum because it is contrary to their *concept of body* (i.e., extension).[1]

In the eyes of Boyle the experimental philosopher, this last argument is worthless. Later, therefore, in his *Continuation of New Experiments* (1669), he tries to determine by means of *experiments* whether there is a Cartesian subtle matter. To that end he takes Descartes' explanation of magnetism and remarks that some modern philosophers explain magnetic force as a result of the air between two magnetic bodies being expelled by the magnetic effluvia, causing the two bodies to draw closer together because the expelled air now presses them toward each other from the other side. Now if it is true, Boyle reasons, that air thus plays a role in magnetism, a magnetic force would have to be much smaller in a vacuum. This he tests by suspending from a magnet a small steel plate with a hook to which a weight is attached—first in the open air, then under the glass receiver of the vacuum pump. The magnet is observed to hold "very near" the same weight each time. "Very near," writes Boyle, for although removing the air cannot be regarded as weakening the actual power of the magnet, yet it must diminish its power to sustain the steel since the weight of the object has now increased by an amount equal to the weight of the displaced air.[2]

In the same work we find "an attempt to examine the motions and sensibility of the Cartesian *Materia subtilis*, or the Aether." Once again Boyle begins by declaring that he does not want to enter into the debate between atomists and Cartesians. He is aware of their speculative arguments, but he wants to try and see whether something can be discovered by way of experiments about the existence and the prop-

---

[1] Ibidem; 37f.

[2] *A Continuation of New Experiments;* 3:238f.

erties of that aether. He arranges to have a bellows fall shut inside a vacuum: a feather attached in front of the opening does not move.[1] This negative result does not, wisely, lead him to conclude that therefore "subtle matter" does not exist, only that he cannot demonstrate its existence.

Thus he sees both the pros and cons. His rationalistic corpuscular theorizing would have him decide against a *vacuum coacervatum*, his experimental empiricism in favor of it. Against the atomists he advances reason, against the Cartesians experiments. He remains undecided and states—as he does more often in his *New Experiments* when he sees no way out—that he will no longer speak about it because the controversy about a vacuum is a metaphysical rather than a physical question.[2] This is the same attitude taken by Pascal's friend Roberval when he said, in a positivist vein, that he would like to send those debates about a vacuum back to the Schools, where they came from.[3]

What experiments cannot decide Boyle leaves undecided, implying a considerable restriction of his rationalism. This is related to what might be called his scepticism. To his mind, the certainty of a science that flows entirely from reason would be complete, but . . . such a science is impossible.[4] And the certainty of a science based on experiments is never complete because it is never finished, and also because experiments are subject to error. Realizing this, one can never accept scientific conclusions without some reservations.

A certain scientific scepticism was not unknown in the Royal Society—not an absolute but a relative scepticism, as a counterpoise to

---

[1] *A Continuation of New Experiments*; 3:250–53.

[2] *New Experiments;* 1:38.

[3] Boyle, however, had not had the opportunity to read Roberval's work; cf. *Against Linus;* 1:120, 124.

[4] Except in mathematics, if one accepts unconditionally that its axioms are correct and our reasoning is indeed faultless. Since no one doubted this in the 17th century, we see how Pascal and Boyle, like Descartes, hold mathematics up as an example of a science with complete certainty, but likewise how both, unlike Descartes, emphasize the big difference between mathematical and scientific certainty.

On Pascal's views of mathematics and science, see my "Pascal, zijn wetenschap en zijn religie," *Orgaan* (1939): 147–78; Eng. trans.: "Pascal, His Science and His Religion," *Free University Quarterly* 2 (1952/53): 106–37. A new translation was recently prepared by Prof. H. Floris Cohen of the University of Twente and published in *Tractrix: Yearbook for the History of Science* 1 (1989): 115–39.

scientific dogmatism,[1] witness the work of Joseph Glanvill, F.R.S., *Scepsis scientifica, or Confessed Ignorance the Way of Science* (1665).

Boyle's *Sceptical Chymist* (1661) breathes the same spirit. It subjects the opinions of scholastics and chemists to the critique of reason, but especially also to the critique of experiment, for, as Boyle says elsewhere, he dares to "speak confidently and positively of very few things, except of matters of fact" and therefore often uses expressions like "perhaps," "it seems," "it is not improbable," or shies away from even "so much as venturing at explications."[2] He does not consider it a weakness in his work that he writes with a measure of uncertainty, for, as Aristotle notes somewhere, "to seem to know all things certainly, and to speak positively of them, is a trick of bold and young fellows."[3]

It would be incorrect to deduce from all this that Boyle was really a sceptic, for in an appendix to his *Sceptical Chymist* he remarks that he does not belong to this sect since they were hardly "less prejudicial to natural philosophy than to divinity itself."[4] Therefore he will not join the genuine sceptics in asserting that to the human understanding all things are doubtful; he proposes doubts "not only with design, but with hope, of being at length freed from them by the attainment of undoubted truth, which I seek, that I may find it."[5] Thus his scepticism is very limited; it is for him a methodical doubt. For he regards truth as "one of the chief of those goods that God has of all others laid the most in common, [so that] any man may make himself a sharer in it." Accordingly, Boyle concludes, "I am glad to find truth in the doctrines of the chemists; but when I cannot discern it there, I choose rather to seek it elsewhere than sit down without it."[6]

It is characteristic of Boyle's scientific scepticism that he looks for a remedy in experiments because reason alone, without the support of deliberate observations, cannot overcome its own doubt.

§ 6. The Nature of Hypotheses

We might well wonder after all this: is Boyle truly of a rationalist mind? In his view, whatever is intelligible is not necessarily true, and

---

[1] Cf. Lechler, *Geschichte des englischen Deismus,* p. 140.

[2] *Physiological Essays;* 1:307.

[3] *New Experiments;* 1:2.

[4] *The Producibleness of Chymical Principles;* 1:591.

[5] Ibidem.

[6] Ibidem.

that which cannot be explained can yet be true! The only genuinely
rationalistic element in his outlook might be his view that at least in
principle everything is intelligible. But as we shall see later, this
statement too needs to be taken with a grain of salt. Nor do we see
Boyle *proceed,* as a strict rationalist would do, from the first principles
of matter and motion, to develop the whole world of phenomena
through logical deduction. Rather, with him the order is reversed: he
explains *a posteriori,* after the facts, rather than *a priori* by predicting
the facts from the theory. But even when he retraces the steps he does
not always end up at the first principles; even then he does not arrive
at a strictly coherent system.

No doubt, says Boyle, the most satisfactory explanations to the
understanding would be those that reduce things to their ultimate
causes, to the most "primitive and catholic affections of matter" (the
bulk, shape and motion of corpuscles). It is a misconception, however,
to think that an explanation is rational only if a phenomenon is reduced
to its ultimate causes. There are various degrees of explanation. In its
most general terms, to explain is to deduce a thing "from something
else in nature more known than itself." Therefore an explanation "from
intermediate causes" is not to be despised but may be considered a true
explanation. If one explains the sinking or floating of an object in terms
of its gravity, which is a universal property of matter, then gravity is
to be regarded as a reason for its behavior, even though in that case the
phenomenon is not deduced from atoms nor has any philosopher
offered a satisfactory explanation of the cause of gravity. Similarly, an
explanation that invokes "spring" is a true explanation, even though
spring itself is not satisfactorily explained.[1]

Before looking further into the nature of Boyle's "intermediate causes,"
we do well to ask, How can he be sure that the mechanistic system is
a valid one? For so long as it is not one large interconnected whole but
consists merely of isolated fragments, one cannot be certain of the
correct foundations. The conclusions drawn from experiments, after all,
being only partial explanations, do not go all the way back to the
foundations. So how can I know for certain that the "mechanical
hypothesis" is valid? Let us first see what demands Boyle makes upon
an hypothesis, and then whether these demands are met in this instance.

The "requisites of a good hypothesis," according to Boyle, are not
only that it be in conformity with the natural phenomenon it is intended
to explain, but also that it "comport fairly" with all other phenomena

---

[1] *Physiological Essays;* 1:308f.

and all other truths. Whoever draws up a theory for all time, therefore, must take care, not only that the facts already noted do not contradict the hypothesis, but also that no phenomena discovered hereafter shall contradict it. It is difficult to construct an accurate hypothesis upon the incomplete history of the phenomena of nature that we have. Many things may be discovered later that are scarcely dreamt of today, and these may well overthrow the very doctrines which at present are "speciously enough accommodated" to the observations made thus far.[1]

Reviewing these demands that Boyle makes upon an hypothesis, we might well fear that the mechanical hypothesis cannot possibly be an hypothesis that has any certainty. For in this line of reasoning the theory is built on induction, and induction is never complete. Boyle speaks of "accommodating" an hypothesis to fit the phenomena. In this line of thinking, therefore, a theory that encompasses *all* facts must be "accommodated" to an immense quantity of factual material.

But this is indeed the case, says Boyle. The mechanical hypothesis, thanks to its internal consistency, has hitherto been able to "explicate things corporeal" without "crossing any known observation or law of nature," and it may therefore be regarded as certain also for the future.[2] That it is sound cannot be demonstrated *a priori* but only by trial. It will probably remain valid, for its principles are, as it were, the letters of the alphabet, and the possibility that a new language should arise which cannot be reduced to the letters of the alphabet is as improbable as that a new physical hypothesis will appear that will overthrow ours.[3]

This last figure of speech reminds us once again that there is no question of a single uniform deduction from the basic mechanical principles. Just as many accounts can be written with the same letters, so the mechanical principles must harbor many possibilities—at least so long as Boyle leaves them that vague and undefined. As well, if he leaves them that vague he can always adjust them to fit the facts or, as he puts it, "accommodate the hypothesis." His very considerable collection of experimental evidence in physics and especially in chemistry affirms him in his belief that everything can be explained in terms of the shape, size, order and motion of material corpuscles and that therefore his hypothesis is sound. But these generalities exhaust the *certainty* of the mechanical hypothesis! Boyle rescues only the *principles* of explanation, the letters of the alphabet, and not the one

---

[1] *The Excellency of Theology;* 4:59.

[2] *The Mechanical Hypothesis;* 4:77.

[3] Ibidem; 78.

system of explanation, the account written with those letters. He refuses to let himself be pressed into the strait-jacket of any one particular mechanico-philosophical system. Thus he leaves his options wide open and instead of considering this vagueness and flexibility a disadvantage he is very pleased that it affords a vast number of variations of special mechanical explanations: he cannot conceive any principle that is more comprehensive or intelligible.[1]

That some facts admit of more than one mechanical explanation, then, is but another reason not to choose between the atomistic and Cartesian standpoints. The "spring of the air" is a good example. The reduction in the volume of the air when it is compressed finds its mechanical "explanation" in its elasticity or spring. But this explanation can "perhaps" be explained further, says Boyle. And then he presents his readers with the choice, either of regarding the air as a collection of flexible particles that are eager to stretch when compressed, or of following the explanation of that "most ingenious gentleman Des Cartes," who asserts that air consists of a mass of flexible particles of various shape and size that float in the aether, each one trying "to beat off all others from coming within the little sphere requisite to its motion." The second explanation is thus more dependent on the motion of the particles than on their size and structure. Now Boyle does not wish to declare himself for either theory, but since the first is somewhat simpler he will henceforward use it.[2]

Having chosen the hypothesis of elastic air particles, he goes on, in his *General History of the Air*, to allow different representations of it, "according to the several contrivances men may devise to answer the phenomena," such as the coiled springs of a watch, or a parcel of curled hairs of wool, or thin, springy wood-shavings, or extremely slender wires or spiral threads. In short, a great variety of "conjectures" are possible.[3] Of course these are only analogies and not causal explanations, but he appeals to the fact that Bacon and even "that severe philosopher" Descartes use images (little eels for water particles and little rigid staves for salt particles) that are more than images since they must be understood as arguments that explain nature by analogy.[4] Using a Baconian term, Boyle calls them "analogous instances."

In Boyle, then, an hypothesis really follows after the facts; it does not provide *the* explanation but one or more plausible representations.

---

[1] *The Mechanical Hypothesis*; 4:69f.
[2] *New Experiments;* 1:12.
[3] *History of the Air;* 5:614.
[4] *The Christian Virtuoso;* 5:511.

He states repeatedly that the corpuscular philosophy *illustrates* the experiments, and he refers to his hypotheses as "conjectures."

Hence one must not make too much of it when Boyle says of a phenomenon that it can be "deduced" from both the atomist and the Cartesian hypothesis.[1] There can be no question of strict deduction here. Thus he says that from either hypothesis one can deduce with great probability ("it can scarce otherwise be") that many bodies give off invisible effluviums. On the atomistic hypothesis, such emanations fly from the body, as all particles are constantly in motion. On the Cartesian hypothesis, bodies lack all innate motion yet have their pores penetrated by a celestial matter which carries some particles off into the air. By these—and perhaps still other—considerations it may be shown *a priori* that there exist extremely minute exhalations, but "it may be as satisfactory, and more useful" to demonstrate it *a posteriori* by particular experiments.[2]

The word satisfactory clearly betrays the experimenter. A rationalist *pur sang* could only be satisfied after coming to certainty through incontrovertible ratiocination.

The particular experiments which Boyle then carries out are done with a very accurate balance, although he cautions that one must make allowance for the fact that the effluvia may be so subtle that the balance fails to register any loss of weight.[3]

Sometimes he is successful in having experiments decide between different corpuscular explications. In the tract *New Experiments to Make Fire and Flame Stable and Ponderable* he juxtaposes the view of the atomists (Gassendi) that fire is corporeal and the view of the Cartesians that it is only a modification of the motion of terrestrial particles caused by the aether. However, declares Boyle in the Preface to the tract, the corporeity of light and fire cannot be determined by "mere ratiocinations" but only by experiments.[4]

On the basis of (misinterpreted) experiments Boyle in this case ends by stating his preference for the atomistic hypothesis, because the calcinated substance has gained weight: particles must have penetrated through the glass and fastened themselves to the heated metal inside the

---

[1] *A Continuation of New Experiments;* 3:278.

[2] Ibidem; 278f.

[3] Ibidem; 280; cf. also *Of the Strange Subtilty of Effluviums;* 3:674.

[4] *Fire and Flame;* 3:707.

vessel.[1] Such penetration may be achieved by fine particles of fire
("igneous corpuscles"), not by vehemently agitated particles of
terrestrial matter.[2] The choice, however, seems to Boyle almost too
definitive: perhaps it is not impossible, he says, to reconcile the
experiments to either of the contending hypotheses by means of "slight
theoretical alterations"![3]

This last suggestion shows again that he does not deduce strictly
from the corpuscular theory but, inversely, accommodates it to the
phenomena. It cannot be denied, however, that the "corpuscular theory
in general" did inspire him to engage in particular experiments; of that
we have already given several examples.

Given the lack of rigor of the hypotheses formulated by Boyle, it
comes as no surprise that he also affirms the validity of working
hypotheses. In physiology, he writes, truth is sometimes discovered by
drawing up an hypothesis to explain a problem and then by examining
to what extent it "solves" the phenomena. Thus the understanding is
sometimes instructed by its own errors, for truth "does more easily
emerge out of error than confusion"[4]—the confusion, that is, if the
facts were left without a theoretical framework. In this connection
Boyle does insist that such a theory (he calls it a "super-structure"!)
should build on a quantity of factual evidence that is proportional to the
range it seeks to cover and that it be looked upon as tentative only—the
best, or the least imperfect, that we have, not the absolutely perfect one
that is to be acquiesced in.[5]

Of course Boyle tries to push his explanations back as far as
possible. The explanation of the reduction in volume of the air from its
elasticity, and the explanation of that elasticity from the spring of the
minutest particles of air, in their turn require an explanation of how the
air particles acquire their spring. This too must be traced back to a
mechanical cause, and here too Boyle sees all kinds of possibilities.
Sometimes he disposes of it with analogies, as we have seen; but at
other times he ventures a causal explanation: he will suggest that
particles of a certain kind may acquire motion as a result of the
"bending" of the elastic corpuscle; or again, he will propose that some

---

[1] Boyle did not realize that part of the air combined with the metal. He did
notice that the air in the glass had decreased, for when he unsealed the vessel
he "heard the outward air rush in." *Fire and Flame*; 3:720.

[2] Ibidem; 729.

[3] Ibidem; 707.

[4] *Physiological Essays;* 1:303.

[5] Ibidem.

subtle ambient matter may be obstructed in its passage through the pores of the spring. But Boyle senses full well that he cannot prove anything, so he ends by stating that he declines to meddle with a subject so difficult of explanation, and which it is not necessary to explain anyway, since the goal of his New Experiments is not to come up with an adequate cause of the spring of the air but only to demonstrate that air does in fact have spring.[1]

Thus, with the aid of his corpuscular philosophy Boyle can only give an imprecise, half finished causal explanation of the elasticity of air. One should not infer, however, that he regards this as a failure of the mechanical hypothesis. In a subsequent tract he makes the observation to Henry More that although he did not "attempt" [*sic*, R.H.] to enter more deeply into the *cause* of that weight and spring, he did prove by his experiments *that* air has weight and spring. And therefore what he offered does deserve to be called a *mechanical* explanation, for no recourse was had to non-physical principles such as a world-soul, *horror vacui,* or the like. Besides, his purpose in this instance was not to give a system of natural philosophy but merely to clarify the phenomena in general.[2]

When his corpuscular theory falls short, therefore, Boyle is content to offer an explanation which is, to be sure, mechanical, but of quite a different sort. To explain aerostatic and hydrostatic phenomena on the analogy of common crude mechanical ones is, after all, markedly different from explaining macroscopic phenomena in terms of microscopic ones.

For that matter, an explanation in terms of corpuscular theory may often do no more than shift the problem. To explain the elasticity of air from elastic particles is of little value if that elasticity is invoked only for this case: that is to say, if not also other, seemingly quite different phenomena can be deduced from it. Short of that, it too is but an analogy, the more so since it involves no mathematical formulation, which can sometimes suggest a relationship between divergent phenomena. How we would have liked to see Boyle later, for example, put a law of elasticity like Hooke's Law as a counterpart to the law we know as Boyle's Law!

Notwithstanding all this, it remains Boyle's ideal, ascending from the phenomena to the causes, to arrive at a truly complete corpuscular

---

[1] *New Experiments;* 1:12.

[2] *An Hydrostatical Discourse Occasioned by the Objections of the Learned Dr. Henry More Against Some Explications of New Experiments made by Mr. Boyle*; 3:608.

theory. Such an all-encompassing theory, however, requires an immense stock of factual material, "a fully competent number of experiments," and that, he believes, is not yet sufficiently available.[1] He himself has often drawn up empirical theories that were soon after "disgraced" by some further or new experiments.[2] Therefore he has contented himself thus far to trace by experiments the "intermediate causes" (to explain something in terms of elasticity or gravity without being able in turn to explain the gravity itself).[3] If particular hypotheses, however, can so readily be invalidated by fresh facts, such will probably be true of general hypotheses as well. Saying this, Boyle does not deny that it can be useful, in order to gratify the intellect, to offer "plausible accounts" of the way in which phenomena might arise from first causes, for this can inspire fresh experimental testing.[4] Evidently, given the state of knowledge of the time, he looks upon an all-encompassing system as no more than a working hypothesis. His expectation, however, is that in the future, when physiological theories will be based on a much larger number of particulars, it will certainly be possible to derive deductions from them that will be unassailable.[5] For the time being, however, Boyle the practical physicist, who sticks to his limited data, gets the better of Boyle the philosopher, who aspires to an all-encompassing system. The schoolmen and Descartes think they have already found it; for Boyle it belongs to the dreams of the future.

With mild sarcasm, Boyle speaks in mock admiration of "great wits" like Aristotle and Campanella who manage from a few general principles to deduce an all-encompassing system. Their theories, he says, are beautiful—at twilight; in the full light of the new experiments they prove to be but delightful fantasies.[6]

> It is not that I at all condemn the practice of those inquisitive wits, that take upon them to explicate to us even the abstrusest phaenomena of nature . . . But I think it is fit for a man to know his own abilities and weaknesses, and not to think himself obliged to imitate all that he thinks fit to praise. I know also that the way to get reputation is to venture to explicate things, and promote opinions;

---

[1] *Physiological Essays;* 1:302f.
[2] Ibidem; 307.
[3] Ibidem; 308f.
[4] Ibidem; 301.
[5] Ibidem; 311.
[6] Ibidem; 302.

for by that course a writer shall be sure to be applauded by one sort of men, and be mentioned by many others; whereas by the way of writing to which I have condemned myself, I can hope for little better . . . than to pass for a drudge of greater industry than reason, and fit for little more than to collect experiments for more rational and philosophical heads to explicate and make use of. But I am content, provided experimental learning be really promoted, [to be but] an under-builder . . . [1]

This modesty is not really sincere, for he fears that all manner of things and properties which are of great practical utility to mankind "would never have been found out *a priori* even by the most profound contemplators," without the diligent examination of particular bodies. The operation of that most useful invention, the magnet, has yet to be explained: it has been discovered "without ascending to the top in the series of causes."[2]

§ 7. Mathematics

To understand the method of a natural scientist it is very important to know what place he assigns in science to mathematics.

Boyle, as he tells us in his treatise *Of the Usefulness of Mathematics,*[3] for a long time, under the influence of Bacon, considered mathematics of little importance for science: mathematics dealt merely with abstract quantity and form; science, by contrast, studied "matter." It was presumably under the influence of physicists like Galileo and Simon Stevinus, who wrote about kinetics, levers and hydrostatics, that he changed his mind on this question. His view of mathematics, then, boils down to this.

Mathematics not only teaches the researcher strict reasoning and deduction, so that he begins to understand what constitutes *proof,* but it is also of direct practical use, especially for experiments in mechanics. To demonstrate the trajectory of a cannon ball Galileo had to be conversant with the nature of a parabola; to calculate planetary motion and eclipses required knowledge of spheres. What wretched theories have been framed and proposed by otherwise keen observers of nature for lack of mathematics: what a pitiful account of dioptrics is offered

---

[1] *Physiological Essays*; 1:307. This was indeed the assessment of August Heller, *Geschichte der Physik* (Stuttgart, 1884), 2:165.

[2] *Physiological Essays;* 1:310.

[3] *The Usefulness of Mathematics*; 3:425–34.

by the Aristotelians in comparison with Kepler, Scheiner and Herrigon!
The working of the eye cannot be understood apart from the properties
of the convex lens of the eye, that is, apart from knowledge of the
properties of convex bodies in general and of the laws of refraction.[1]

The "soul of mathematics," however, is the theory of proportions;
the Fifth Book of Euclid's *Elements,* which deals with this doctrine,
may prove more instructive to the scientist than the Fifth Book of
Aristotle's *Physics.* We apply proportion to motion, as in deducing the
laws of falling bodies. Mathematics saves us many an experiment; if
one wishes to know the length of a pendulum required for a specified
duration of its swing, then anyone unacquainted with the theory of
proportion must find this out by *trial and observation,* but by applying
proportionality one may *deduce* the required length from the length and
time of the swing of another pendulum. Furthermore, the laws of the
refraction and reflection of light enable us by means of mathematical
deduction to solve many other problems, needing but few observations.[2]

Thus Boyle realizes that a mathematical, quantitative treatment of
the phenomena elevates science from a jumble of facts to a system.
However, he is conscious at the same time that ultimately the instances
cited yield mathematical rules, not causal explanations.

According to Boyle, some phenomena in nature are still far from
being explained causally. Yet they can be sharply formulated with the
aid of mathematics through its theory of proportions. Example: the
distance travelled by a falling body is directly proportional to the square
of the time of its fall.[3]

Most theorems and problems of hydrostatics, he says in his
Hydrostatical Paradoxes, are pure productions of reason applied to
things. Archimedes, Stevinus and Galileo studied hydrostatics more as
mathematicians than as philosophers (that is, as "naturalists" or
physicists), without referring the facts to an *explication* of the phenomena.[4]

And indeed, the founders of mechanics, rather than giving causal
explanations or answering the question of why or how, really offered
the mathematical law of the phenomena. In describing their observations they drew up mathematical formulas that were not discovered
strictly empirically; they offered rather an "ideal" mechanics which can

---

[1] *The Usefulness of Mathematics;* 3:426, 428–30.
[2] Ibidem; 430–32.
[3] Ibidem; 431.
[4] *Hydrostatical Paradoxes;* 2:739f.

be no more than *approximated* in an experiment. Thus Boyle sees correctly that their method is analogous to that of mathematics. Not that he personally insists on a *causal* (read: corpuscular) explanation of the laws and phenomena of mechanics (with or without the aid of mathematics). The contrast he makes, rather, is that the writers he quotes approach mechanics (and hydrostatics and pneumatics) from the angle of *"geometry,"* whereas he approaches these fields from the point of view of *experimental physics*.

For this reason he holds a brief to his mathematical readers on behalf of physical experiments in hydrostatics and pneumatics. The mathematicians, Boyle anticipates, will have two objections. The first objection is that his proofs are based on physical tests that do not always demonstrate the thing that is to be demonstrated with mathematical certainty and accuracy.[1]

Boyle answers this by saying that in problems of physics approximate determinations are often sufficient. For that matter, the mathematicians themselves work with approximations in their study of hydrostatics, for the surface of water, strictly speaking, is not level but spherical, and two vertical lines really intersect at the center of the earth.

The second objection is more serious, according to Boyle. It protests that experiments are not needed to confirm explanations, because if the reasoning is strict it cannot but convince every rational human being about matters hydrostatical.[2]

Boyle's rebuttal runs as follows. In pure mathematics, strict demonstration without consulting experience suffices; the postulates on which the demonstration rests are universally accepted as necessary. But in physical enquiries a mistake in assumptions is possible and in that case even if we do not doubt the correctness of the reasoning we will doubt the conclusion because we doubt the starting point. We must, then, consult our senses about the things that fall under its scope, and examine by experiments whether we made any mistakes in our hypotheses or in our reasoning. Even a man like Stevinus, the chief of the modern writers on hydrostatics, thought fit to append some mechanical experiments to confirm the truth of his mathematical proofs.[3] Thus Boyle's refutation essentially amounts to his basic maxim that the strictest reasoning can be overthrown by a single fact to the contrary.

---

[1] Ibidem: 741.

[2] Ibidem.

[3] Ibidem; 742.

§ 8. Mathematics and Experimental Science

Boyle's own contribution to the application of mathematics to natural science is very small. His novel experiments merely confirmed laws found by others, or he conducted experiments that are of a qualitative nature. He did not draw up any purely descriptive mathematical laws of the type of the law of refraction, and even less did he arrive at deductive laws of the type of the law of falling bodies or the law of impact.[1]

His scientific method is absolutely not suited to draw up *a priori,* by way of formal mathematical reasoning proceeding from given axioms, a law as that of free falling bodies. Boyle is too attached to real observation to be able to formulate an ideal law. In this connection it is interesting to note that his only objection to Pascal's *Traité* is that it describes experiments that are not really doable,[2] "mental experiments" in other words. Experiments of that sort, of course, are always perfectly exact; they are visually represented deductions.

But might Boyle not have discovered the same mathematical formulas as Galileo and Stevinus *purely on the basis of experiments?*[3] By approximation, yes, but then there would still have been a big difference. If one discovers hydrostatic laws by means of mathematical deduction, experiments can provide approximate confirmation afterwards. If the results are not exact, one can always blame it on errors in the experiments, thus leaving the law unimpaired. But if one bases himself exclusively on experiments and one does not yet know the law, then it is highly doubtful that it will ever be discovered from the experimental data alone, and if it is discovered approximately, uncertainty remains as to which part of the deviation must be ascribed to error, and which part must be attributed to a possible lack of strict validity of the law.

It will be objected: But what about Boyle's Law? Does Boyle not make *independent* use there of the "soul of mathematics,"

---

[1] It goes almost without saying that Boyle could never bring himself to offer a mathematical "metaphysical" explanation. An attempt such as that of Kepler to discover the ground plan of the universe by means of mathematical speculations (see my "Het Hypothesebegrip van Kepler," *Orgaan* (1939), at p. 49) was reckoned by him among the "extravagant opinions." *The Usefulness of Mathematics;* 3:426.

[2] *Hydrostatical Paradoxes;* 2:746. Some of Pascal's experiments are "easily supposed by a mathematician" but "more ingenious than practicable." Ibidem.

[3] On Galileo, see E. J. Dijksterhuis, *Val en worp* (Groningen, 1924).

proportionality, even while to him that law is of a *purely empirical* nature? We must concede this last point; there is here no deduction from the corpuscular theory, as the kinetic gas theory would offer later, nor a deduction from analogy with the laws of elasticity. Presumably Boyle might never have arrived at the quantitative determination of the relation between pressure and volume if Richard Townley had not given him the idea that this might just be a case of inverse proportionality.[1] He had investigated the pressure of gas only to prove, in opposition to Linus, that a gas is subject to much greater changes in pressure than Linus supposed.

Now it is true that in the course of this investigation he did in fact come upon series of numbers that gave occasion for stating that pressure times volume is constant.[2] Yet Boyle himself remarks that the results are not precise, and then he hesitates whether he should ascribe the deviation to possible errors in the experiments (which he enumerates) or to the invalidity of the law.

If he had first discovered the law himself by deduction before beginning his experiments, just as he had been acquainted with the partially deductive laws of mechanics of Stevinus and others before investigating those experimentally, he would not have dropped it that easily. But Boyle does not aim at an ideal and formal science of nature, but at an empirical and representational-explanatory one. He comes at the law from the standpoint of experimentation and mentions the mathematical formula, in spite of the observed deviations from it, only because he has no idea of the magnitude of his experimental errors. If his instruments had had the precision of today, he would not even have come to any mathematical formulation.

---

[1] "I had not reduced the trials I had made about measuring the expansion of the air to any certain hypothesis, when that ingenious gentleman Mr. Richard Townley was pleased to inform me, that having by the perusal of my physico-mechanical experiments been satisfied that the spring of the air was the cause of it, he endeavoured . . . to supply what I had omitted concerning the reducing to a precise estimate, how much air dilated of itself loses of its elastical force, according to the measures of its dilatation." *Against Linus;* 1:160. But Townley's measurements were too inaccurate to confirm his hypothesis. Boyle's measurements as well as those of Dr. Henry Power and Lord Brouncker (ibidem; 1:155, 160) confirmed Townley's theory not too badly. Ernst Gerland, *Geschichte der Physik* (Leipzig, 1892), is wrong in minimizing Townley's contribution in favor of Boyle's.

[2] Boyle does not provide a single mathematical formula; even his gas law he formulates verbally: "the hypothesis that supposes the pressures and expansions to be in reciprocal proportion." *Against Linus;* 1:158.

It seems to us that this is also the explanation of the curious fact that in his enumeration of the applications of proportionality Boyle mentions everything except his own gas law, and in the second place, that he never mentions the gas law again later, not even as an experimental result. After all, he had not deduced the law with mathematical rigor, nor had he discovered it with perfect exactness through experimental induction. Boyle the experimenting physicist remained uncertain and so he published his tables of pressures and volumes and left it at that, without ever returning to this law as a law of mathematical certainty.

Boyle's method is therefore quite different from Galileo's. Yet, as our quotations show, he had good insight into "the method of the mathematicians" and could appreciate it too. It is disappointing, therefore, that he did not fix the analogy between the elasticity of a watch-spring and of a gas in a mathematically formulated law of elasticity. But neither did he test experimentally the hypothesis of the springlike particles of air by quantitatively determining the compressibility of an actual quantity of watch-springs and comparing it with that of air, something that would certainly have been in his line.

Likewise do we look in vain for a causal, corpuscular explanation in mathematical garb. We might briefly expect that, for Boyle makes the remark that mathematics is "of considerable use" not only to the applied and experimental "physiologist" but also to the "speculative naturalist"; after all, material bodies have shape and size and therefore fall under geometry, even as they also have motion.[1] But our hope that Boyle will now proceed with a rigorously mathematical treatment of the corpuscular theory is dashed. When he begins to describe the shape and motion of corpuscles all we get is vague analogies and images.

If we remind ourselves once again, however, that Boyle, for all his corpuscular theory, comes at physics and chemistry *from the angle of experimentation,* then this deficiency becomes quite understandable. As an experimenter he is unable to offer a direct demonstration of corpuscles, and—in part owing to this circumstance—his causal explanations are ever *plausible,* never compelling. Thus he is unable to provide a mathematical-*causal* treatment of the corpuscular theory analogous to the mathematical-*descriptive* one in hydrostatics. In hydrostatics he was able, on the basis of unmistakable facts (and with a bit of a dare as regards experimental errors), to discover by induction the mathematico-mechanical "hypothesis" (which he had already inherited, however, from the "mathematicians," who had obtained it by deduction), and from it to deduce new phenomena. With respect to

---

[1] *The Usefulness of Mathematics;* 3:427.

corpuscles he does not have experimentally verified facts at his disposal and for that reason he feels powerless to apply—as the kinetic theory of gases would do later—the laws of impact and motion to corpuscles and from these to deduce further phenomena. He does state, however, that the laws of mechanics hold not only for large bodies but also for small invisible ones.[1] The application of this proposition he leaves to posterity!

Whenever science is approached from the experimental angle, a high degree of precision is usually desired. Thus the laws of the refraction and reflection of light, which admit of such simple mathematical formulations, may be verified by comparing precise observations. Sometimes, however, the progress of science is not promoted by too much caution in drawing conclusions or by too much precision in conducting experiments. Ignoring the scruples entertained by Boyle himself, we may safely say that precisely the crudeness of the experimental method led to the general acceptance of the equation that pressure times volume is constant.

The kinetic theory of gases, which proceeded from equally "ideal" assumptions as did the mechanics of Galileo and others, discovered the same law deductively. Subsequent to this, experiments were carried out with far greater precision; it was then noted that Boyle's Law could not be verified and that the deviations could definitely not be attributed to experimental errors. Had Boyle's Law not been known beforehand, these very exact observations would probably not have led to it either. The results of the measurements could then be expressed only in an empirical formula found by series expansion. This was in fact done by Regnault.[2]

Nevertheless, because of the kinetic theory of gases Boyle's Law had become an "ideal" that people could not relinquish, and so we see Van der Waals,[3] on the basis of supplementary hypotheses, formulating a corrected version of "the law of Boyle" that was likewise "explanatory" in character and not purely empirical.

Thus it is possible that the same relatively simple "ideal" laws which (proceeding from one or more axioms) are discovered deductively, would be discovered on a purely experimental basis only if the experiments are not too accurate. If in an experimental approach to physics one shrinks from simplification, one usually arrives at empirical

---

[1] *The Mechanical Hypothesis;* 4:71.

[2] *Mémoires de l'Académie des Sciences* XXI (Paris, 1847), p. 419.

[3] Cf. J. D. van der Waals, *Over de continuiteit van den gas- en vloeistof-toestand* (doctoral thesis; Leyden, 1873), p. 56.

formulas serviceable only to description and calculation, without laying bare the interconnection of the phenomena.

The most fruitful approach is to come at nature from both the "mathematical" and the "empirical" angles. Since one can never have *a priori* certainty with respect to axioms in natural science, if one sticks only to deduction a science will result that has lost all contact with reality. But if one sticks only to induction a description will result—if need be, a description framed in mathematical formulas—that lacks all conceptualization.

There is no doubt that Boyle realized that a strict empiricism is impossible and that a strictly rational science is just as impossible. He upholds the distinct character of natural science as against mathematics. Sometimes he argues from experiment to hypothesis, at other times from hypothesis to experiment, in this way combining induction and deduction. He would be an ideal type of experimental physicist if he did not on occasion carry his methodological scepticism too far. He knows too well that experiments entail errors and that agreement between theory and experience can never be complete. This keeps him sometimes from making positive pronouncements. The gas law is posited weakly; during his inquiry into the elements he has renewed doubts about tentatively treating as an element a substance which he cannot analyze. One could wish for a greater degree of positiveness in his treatment of the phenomena.

Although Boyle states that mathematics is requisite for the concepts of corpuscular philosophy because corpuscles possess shape, size and motion, he nevertheless—as we noted above—draws no deductions from this. Quite in keeping with all his "explications," the size, shape and motion of the particles in each phenomenon are afterwards assumed to be such that the phenomenon *could* follow from them. His corpuscular images—hooked, round, snakelike particles—only serve to make graphic how the phenomenon might possibly have come about.

The value Boyle attaches to graphic representation is most apparent in chemistry. Here again there is no question of predicting the phenomena. For example, the fact that gold and mercury, following all kinds of chemical manipulations, re-emerge unimpaired and undiminished he afterwards makes "intelligible" by assuming these metals to be made up of "strongly coherent" secondary particles.[1] But he is unsure whether those secondary particles will survive every other reaction. The absence of the modern "analytical" concept of element causes his chemical explanations to lack fixed points to which all changes can be related and allows them to shift in all directions.

---

[1] *The Mechanical Hypothesis;* 4:76.

Chemical theory of the 19th century was based on Dalton's atomic theory which, because of its connection with Lavoisier's concept of element, had a much more "predictive" character than Boyle's. Drawing up formulas and reaction equations enabled scientists not only to explain afterward but also to surmise beforehand. Dalton's atoms were no more directly demonstrated than Boyle's corpuscles, yet atomic theory because of its graphic nature had a firmer hold on chemists than the abstract "thermodynamic" interpretation. Similarly Boyle's corpuscles provide our imagination with more of a handle than do the substantial forms of the scholastics, and for this reason his method of "explanation" had a positive effect on the growth of scientific chemical research. Scientists got a sense that they were no longer facing unsolvable enigmas.

"To explain is to deduce a thing from something more known than itself," says Boyle, and apparently he considers the phenomena of mechanics "more known" than the capricious phenomena that we encounter especially in chemistry but also in physics (light, magnetism). In point of fact, however, to explain is for Boyle not so much to deduce from something more *known* as to deduce from something more *familiar*. For his corpuscular explanations only shift the problem: a phenomenon is deduced from the mechanical properties of the corpuscles, but these in turn must be explained mechanically, and so forth.

Now even if these explanations were actually correct rather than merely "conjectural," they would not for that reason be completely intelligible. It is more graphic but no more intelligible if the motion of a corpuscle is ascribed to its collision or impact with another corpuscle rather than to the effective operation of a world-soul or some other immaterial principle. No more than we can understand how a spirit moves matter can we conceive a collision as truly intelligible. That Boyle realized this full well becomes clear when he pillories the pride of certain mechanical philosophers; then he points to the fact that the fundamental principles of mechanics transcend our intellect.[1]

---

[1] See also below, p. 87. Boyle does not really have the right, therefore, to accuse scholasticism of inconsistency when it turns to mathematical laws instead of substantial forms to explain the refraction of light. For scholasticism distinguishes between causal explanation (by means of substantial forms, among other things) and mathematical description; see my "Het Hypothesebegrip van Kepler," *Orgaan* (1939), p. 40. In practice, Boyle has this distinction as well; only, with him the causal explanation is mechanistic. The Schoolmen with their "obscure" principles are unable to offer satisfactory causal explanations, but neither can Boyle quite carry it off with his "plain" principles. Scholasticism

What we can say is this: Boyle "explains" in terms of principles that are usually more familiar and graphic than the phenomena to be explained; scholasticism "explains" in terms of principles that are more derived from philosophical reflection than from immediate experience and are therefore less "familiar." Boyle searches in every instance for physical causes; scholasticism resorts too quickly to metaphysical causes. Boyle at least recognizes that his explaining is very deficient; scholasticism actually supposes it has understood the phenomena by giving them erudite labels.

It should not be held against Boyle that he looks for "explanation" exclusively in the mechanical sphere. Galileo, Huygens, in fact even Newton, do the same, and most nineteenth-century researchers look upon a mechanical explanation of nature as the ultimate ideal. But it is a weakness in Boyle that he is content to have the mechanical theory "accommodate itself" to the phenomena and be so flexible that it can give more than one explanation to "illustrate" the same fact. His corpuscular theory is a tree that bears too much fruit, with the result that not one reaches full maturity.

Only if the corpuscular theory were dressed in mathematical garb would it become sharper and achieve more. Boyle is too weak and too dependent a mathematician to hazard such a venture.

It should also be remembered, however, that the development of the foundations of mechanics and higher mathematics was still ongoing, with the result that the necessary tools were in part lacking. Christian Huygens, like Boyle a fervent champion of the corpuscular theory, would have been the obvious person to perform that task, both on account of his superior knowledge of mechanics (such as the law of impact) and because of his much greater mathematical talent. He never got around to it; not until Daniel Bernoulli and his kinetic theory of *gases* (1738) was the first step taken in this direction. A gas theory covers only a limited area; no one has ever come up with an all-encompassing, purely mechanico-mathematical atomistic explanation of nature.

§ 9. A Comparison with Other Natural Philosophers

a. Boyle and Descartes
René Descartes (1596–1650) and Robert Boyle are both of the opinion that all things find their cause in matter and motion. Against the teleology of scholasticism they posit the mechanical-causal interpreta-

---

therefore has just as much a right to mathematical description alongside causal explanation.

tion as the only correct one. But directly in working this out they part ways. Descartes would dispute the truth of *all* teleology; Boyle wants to bar it only from natural science proper: in his reflections in "natural philosophy" he certainly acknowledges the reality of final causes.

Descartes is a true rationalist who supposes he can deduce the phenomena by proceeding from basic principles which to him are as certain as those of geometry (in his day still regarded as absolutely certain) and by following a process of reasoning which is as certain as mathematical reasoning. Reason is the sole means of knowing; it contains in principle everything needed to acquire complete knowledge of the world. All one need do is apply it correctly. In essence Descartes' system is deductive; it claims the certainty of mathematics; experiments may at most confirm *a posteriori* what is known to Reason *a priori*. In truth, if experience were to show the contrary, Descartes would still trust reason more than the senses: "The demonstrations of all this are so certain that even if experience would seem to show us the contrary we would nevertheless be obliged to attach greater credence to our reason than to our senses." Boyle by contrast says that rational philosophers scruple not to alter or renounce their opinions "when once they find them contradicted by experience."[1] He grants experimentation pride of place; he is after all a disciple of Bacon, who insists that one must not think up but *find out* how nature works.[2]

Descartes honors the rationalistic method; he thinks that his deduction has "greater certitude than morality." Boyle follows the "historical" empirical method and therefore attains only "moral certainty."[3]

Descartes is absolutely certain about the foundations of mechanical philosophy because in themselves they are evident to reason. Boyle is equally sure of them, but only because experiments never contradict them.[4]

To be sure, Boyle too aspires after an all-encompassing system, but he wants to secure it by induction; he is far removed from the philosophical hubris of Descartes, and he has not yet advanced to the scientific hubris of the 19th century. Descartes believes he has in principle reconstructed the system of the universe; his expectation is that posterity will broaden, not deepen it. Boyle joins Bacon in assuming the endless progress of science. As long as science is in-

---

[1] *The Christian Virtuoso;* 5:538.

[2] *The History of Cold;* 2:462.

[3] Cf. below, p. 87.

[4] Cf. above, p. 30.

complete, more than one rational explanation is available to inductive researchers, so that there can be no question with Boyle of a truly rationalistic deductive system. He pokes fun at "those heroic wits" who from a few basic principles manage to deduce all phenomena. He says that it is one thing to offer a general theory covering all phenomena in terms of the shape, size and motion of corpuscles, quite another to be able to say which particular form, size and motion of the atoms produce the effects to be explained.[1] Even when it reasons back from the experiments to the intermediate causes, reason still sees different possibilities, and even then it remains true that "our dim reason" cannot determine which of the several possible ways nature has made use of.[2]

Descartes' cosmological system, however much it may appear in our eyes to be a product of his imagination, is to him the interpretation of reality discovered by Reason. Boyle's corpuscular theories, too, spring from his imagination, but he is aware that he is using his imagination; in his eyes they merely offer *possible* explanations; they are mere "illustrations." Generally speaking, they are not even deductions that he puts side by side with induction; here he does not hesitate whether to experiment or to deduce, but whether "to investigate or to guess."[3]

Descartes and Boyle both say they are convinced that everything is intelligible. A deductive world system, however, requires not only that everything is intelligible *in principle,* but also that whatever is intelligible is in fact comprehended, hence explained. In contrast to Descartes, Boyle does not believe that everything can be explained. He accepts the empirically given world, in regard to which he cannot perceive rationally why it is the way it is and why it has the laws it has. He accepts the fundamental principles because experience forces him to do so, not because reason alone compels him. In this way his rationalism is greatly limited by his empiricism.

b. Boyle and Gassendi

Boyle does not, like Descartes, wish to "speak too quickly of the true and adequate causes" but would rather, with certain modern ("Epicurean") philosophers, assign "not precisely the true but the possible causes" of the phenomena to be explained.[4] This association of Boyle with the Gassendists is not without its deeper cause! A sharp contrast

---

[1] *Against Hobbes;* 1:195. *Physiological Essays;* 1:309.

[2] *The Usefulness of Natural Philosophy;* 2:45.

[3] *The Excellency of Theology;* 4:49.

[4] *The Usefulness of Natural Philosophy;* 2:45.

existed between the mechanistic philosophers Pierre Gassendi (1592–1655) and Descartes. Descartes is willing to argue from principles to phenomena only via reason; Gassendi reserves a large role for the imagination. His causality is a "representational causality," not a strictly logical one. And what else are Boyle's "corpuscularian explications" but graphic representations of how things just might be on the basis of established principles? That he believes those principles of mechanical philosophy to be "clear and distinct" does not mean for him that he *comprehends* what matter and motion are—in fact, he denies this vigorously[1]—but only that he considers them realistic principles of explanation as compared to the hollow terms of non-mechanical systems. To a large extent, they are clear and distinct because they are graphic!

If Boyle thus has in common with Gassendi the basic feature of his method of explanation, so likewise in the explanation of details his agreement each time with Gassendi appears much greater than with Descartes, even if he does not always choose sides. Further, he shares with Gassendi a moderate degree of scientific scepticism and a tendency, despite rationalistic traits, to delimit the human understanding.

Duhem, taking off from Pascal's distinction between *l'esprit fort, mais étroit* and *l'esprit ample, mais faible*,[2] has tried to show that the Continental mind in general is "strong but narrow," aiming for a strict, rational, abstract science, whereas the English in general have a mind that is "broad but weak," capable of taking in many things at once and illustrating the phenomena with graphic, plausible models, not flinching from drawing more than one picture for the selfsame phenomenon or mutually contradictory pictures for different phenomena (think of Lord Kelvin!). Duhem argues that Descartes is predominantly "strong-minded" and Gassendi, though also a Frenchman, "broad-minded," and that therefore a difference in the view of knowledge was bound to arise between them.[3]

Whatever one may think of Duhem's typology, from our analysis of Boyle's view of science it has become abundantly clear that he has the "broad mind" typical of the Englishman. He is not "strong-minded" enough to try and deduce the phenomena from the motion of corpuscles

---

[1] See below, pp. 87, 106.

[2] Pascal, *Pensées,* nr. 2.

[3] *Author's gloss for the English edition:* This paragraph needs some revision. The matter is more complicated; Duhem's distinction is too simple, Pascal's verdict too vague.

by mathematical calculation and the application of the laws of mechanics, as was attempted by the Continental scholars Huygens, Leibniz and Bernoulli. He is certainly not "strong-minded" enough to arrive at a mathematical-causal explanation (or description) of the phenomena according to the method of Newton, who omitted concrete physical representations altogether. If he had possessed enough mathematical talent it would have fitted his scientific type to express every series of observations in a so-called empirical formula.

c. Boyle and Newton
Although Sir Isaac Newton (1643–1727) does not deny that everything in nature might be explained mechanically, he agrees with Boyle that such explanations are still uncertain—and for that very reason disagrees with Boyle that they are of much use. Boyle attaches great value to mechanical explanations in spite of their uncertainty, because he feels the need of concrete representations. Newton, who has a far greater capacity for abstract thinking, feels this need much less so. He did, however, make attempts at corpuscularian explanations, for example of gravity, although he did not publish any explanations of that type. He writes Boyle (in 1679) that his ideas about that are not yet settled, for in natural philosophy "there is no end of fancying." Communicating some "suppositions" and "conjectures" that might explain certain physical properties from mechanical causes, he apologizes to Boyle that his ideas are "so indigested," concluding that "I have so little fancy to things of this nature, that had not your encouragement moved me to it, I should never, I think, have thus far set pen to paper about them."[1]

At the time of his first publication in 1672, *A New Theory of Light and Colours,* Newton declines to say what light really *is;* he does not wish to "mingle conjectures with certainties." Similarly we look in vain in his main work of 1687, *Philosophiae Naturalis Principia Mathematica,* for a physico-causal explanation of gravity, for his declaration, "hypotheses non fingo," (I do not dream up hypotheses) is indeed made in reference to the latter.

Like Boyle, Newton is an advocate of inductive science; however, on the basis of painstaking induction he does arrive at a few general concepts and propositions (which we would not hesitate to call hypotheses), which in turn, when taken as his starting point, enable him mathematically to deduce—and if need be predict—the phenomena. The

---

[1] Newton to Boyle, 28 Feb. 1679; *Life;* 1:cxii–cxvii.

"forces" that he uses to explain them are, he says, "mathematical" and not physical causes.[1]

Boyle nowhere mentions Newton in his works, although he knew him quite well. There are probably several reasons for this. First, when Boyle discussed the methods of the mathematicians (in his *Hydrostatical Paradoxes* of 1666) Newton had not yet published anything; secondly, because of its abstract mathematical quality Newton's work must have been quite foreign to him; finally, a work like the *Principia,* containing as it does mostly mathematics and astronomy, deals precisely with that branch of science which attracted Boyle least and which in his eyes was least useful for his teleological reflections designed to discover God's wisdom through his works. In conclusion it should be noted here as well that although Newton debarred final causes from science in the narrow sense, as Boyle had done, he did, again like Boyle, view them as being actualized in nature.

d. Boyle and Bacon

There is no doubt that Boyle owed his predilection for empirical research to Sir Francis Bacon (1561-1626). However, he followed his hero on one point only, namely that an extensive body of facts—a natural history—must be considered an indispensable foundation for a reliable science of nature. Wisely, he did not adopt Bacon's inductive *method.*[2]

He seldom uses the Baconian terminology (instances, idols, etc.). Nor does he follow Bacon in recommending an *experimentum crucis*[3] for determining whether an hypothesis is correct. According to Bacon, if in the case of two competing hypotheses the experiment confirms the conclusions from the one and not the other, then the rule of geometry holds: the former is held to be correct. Boyle by contrast admits increasingly more suppositions than the ones he suggests himself. He

---

[1] On Newton's method, see H. J. E. Beth, *Newton's Principia* (Groningen, 1932), pt. I, cap. 1; pt. II, cap. 20 and 28.

[2] On this, see Walter Frost, *Bacon und die Naturphilosophie* (Munich, 1927). Frost points out that Bacon's induction is not the contrary of deduction; it is something quite different from induction in Aristotle or J. S. Mill; it is an "interpretation of nature" (p. 74). For that matter, Bacon's "inductive method" remained unfinished. In theory of knowledge the final word has not yet been spoken about the nature of induction.

[3] Cf. Pierre Duhem, *La théorie physique* (2d ed.; Paris, 1914), p. 286.

is much too cautious and fears he has not exhausted every conceivable explanation.[1]

Boyle also managed to emancipate himself from Bacon's bias against Galileo's mathematical deduction and to perceive the usefulness of mathematics for formulating the lawlike behavior of phenomena, even though he did not use it himself.

Doubtless as well, it is under the influence of Bacon that Boyle rigorously separates theology and philosophy from science and keeps natural science free of final causes. In Bacon's opinion, mixing science and religion leads to a heretical religion and a fantastical science[2]; final causes, according to him, belong in metaphysics: "the moment final causes enter the realm of physics they ruin it utterly."[3]

e. Boyle and Pascal

Blaise Pascal (1623–62) is more positivistic than Boyle. Boyle considers corpuscular theories to be "conjectures" of great moment, even though final certainty is still very remote. Pascal does believe that everything arises from "configuration and motion" but to say *which* would be "useless and uncertain." He sticks to the facts, without introducing graphic pictures. Pascal wishes only to offer a descriptive classification of the phenomena. So does Boyle, but as a typical Englishman he also wants to be able to picture to himself how they come about.

Induction, of course, is never complete; we can never be certain that we have based our conclusions on every possible case; to every statement based on induction we must always tacitly add: "insofar as we know"; it never has a rationally compelling necessity; it will always have to be accepted with a certain degree of scepticism. Nevertheless we need to adopt a positive attitude and for the time being act as though the conclusion is certain, if our scientific activity is not to be inhibited.

---

[1] When it is a question, however, of determining whether "pulsion" or "traction" is the cause of change in the level of a barometer when climbing a mountain, Boyle, citing Bacon, refers to Pascal's trial as an "*experimentum crucis*." It is evident from his discussion, however, that at this point he confuses a proof for the "weight" of the air with a proof for the "spring" of the air. *Against Linus;* 1:151.

[2] Francis Bacon, *De dignitate et augmentis scientiarum*, III, 2; *Novum Organum*, Bk. I, Aph. LXV.

[3] Francis Bacon, *De dignitate et augmentis scientiarum*, III, 4; cf. Kuno Fischer, *Francis Bacon und seine Schule*, pp. 221–29.

Now it is curious that Pascal, who is so much more sceptical than Boyle, is nevertheless more positivistic than he in his scientific method. He states: "Diamond is the hardest substance," and then he goes on to say that, of course, we must add: "of those we know."[1] Pascal does not assume, so long as he cannot demonstrate it to the senses, that any matter is present in a vacuum. Boyle wavers here; because of his scepticism he cannot bring himself to make even a tentative pronouncement; for even though he cannot, to be sure, demonstrate anything to be there and accordingly must infer a space devoid of *air,* nevertheless something may yet be discovered in the Torricellian vacuum! Moreover, without matter he cannot conceive the propagation of light. That is a rationalistic argument and Pascal would have disposed of it with his dictum that "it is not by our capacity to conceive things that we should judge of their truth."[2] And Boyle no doubt would have conceded the point.[3]

We have already remarked that Boyle looks to experiments as a remedy for his scientific methodological scepticism. But this, assuming an inductive approach, will not avail without a good measure of positivism. A good illustration of this is the definition of an element. Lavoisier defines an element as "the final limit that analysis arrives at"; the element may well be a compound, but relative to our experiments and observations it behaves like a simple substance and as long as it does so we must regard it as such.[4] In Boyle's definition, an element is "a substance *which is perfectly homogeneous* and which is not further resoluble into any number of distinct substances."[5]

It boggles the mind to hear this definition referred to again and again as "our" modern definition.[6] Boyle calls a substance an "element" when it is, in the strict sense of the word, simple. The first requirement that he posits automatically implies the second: an absolute element, obviously, cannot be further analyzed by chemical means. The order of these requirements cannot be reversed, for once he has the absolute concept of element in view the "sceptical chemist" can never be content with the outside limit of analysis, since there is no guarantee

---

[1] On Pascal's scientific method, see my "Pascal, His Science and His Religion," *Tractrix* 1 (1989): 115–39.

[2] *De l'esprit géométrique*, Harvard Classics ed. (1910), p. 439.

[3] *Things Above Reason;* 4:422; cf. below, pp. 107, 125.

[4] A. L. Lavoisier, *Traité élémentaire de chimie,* I (2d ed.; Paris, 1793), p. xvii.

[5] *The Sceptical Chymist;* 1:530; see also ibidem; 511, 531; emphasis added.

[6] Cf. my *Het Begrip element,* pp. 201–5.

that future analysis will not make further progress. And even if it were
certain that analysis had reached the uttermost limits of human
capabilities, the possibility would still remain that the composite nature
of the unanalyzable substances might be discovered in some other way.

Boyle does mention gold as an example of something which on
account of its solid texture might be an element, yet he also thinks he
has found a means to transmute it into another metal.[1] And he submits
that, even if there are substances whose texture can be destroyed
neither by fire nor by the "usual agents employed by chemists," yet it
would not necessarily follow that they are elementary, since such agents
may yet be found![2] It remains an open question for Boyle, therefore,
whether we actually know any elements, in fact "whether there be a
necessity to admit any elements . . . at all"![3] Once again his too great
caution prevented him from attaining positive results.

---

[1] Cf. *An Historical Account of a Degradation of Gold Made by an Anti-Elixir:
A Strange Chemical Narrative* 4:371–78.

[2] *The Sceptical Chymist;* 1:579.

[3] Ibidem; 562.

Chapter III

RELIGION AND THE STUDY OF NATURE

§ 1. The Conflict Between Science and Theology

It did not escape Boyle's notice that there was a growing opposition in his day between the practitioners of natural philosophy and the adherents of religion. Already in one of his earliest works he observed that scientists and physicians alike, especially if they held to the atomistic philosophy, "inclined to atheism, or at least to an unconcernedness for any particular religion."[1] But also at the end of his life he deplored the rapid growth of irreligion, "especially among those that aspire to pass for wits, and several of them too for philosophers."[2]

Conversely, theologians believed that a Christian could not pursue science without harm to his faith. In 1665 Boyle wrote to the presbyterian minister Richard Baxter that he was glad "you are none of those narrow-souled divines, that, by too much suspecting natural philosophy, tempt many of its votaries to suspect theology."[3]

The situation, therefore, was that "the libertines thought a virtuoso [scientist] ought not to be a Christian, and the others [who defended religion], that he could not be a true one."[4]

The same scientific hubris that we know from the 19th century also affected many of Boyle's contemporaries. They nurse the fallacy that only those things are certain which lie within reach of their science, and at the same time they have a tendency (also known to us from the 19th century) to extend the scope of science illicitly by presenting as established facts preconceptions which they borrow from

---

[1] *The Style of Holy Scripture;* 2:253.

[2] *The Christian Virtuoso;* 5:508.

[3] *Letters;* 6:520.

[4] *The Christian Virtuoso;* 5:508.

a materialistic philosophy. Religion in particular is the antipode of "science" in their eyes: religion is founded on the imagination of an overheated brain; science is based on reality perceived by cool minds with the aid of the senses. They try to act as though they represent "*the* world of science," while in actual fact they are nothing but investigators of lesser rank: the truly great scientists are usually more modest!

Boyle has the merit of having unmasked these false pretensions. He unmasks their pride: "There is scarce any sort of learned men, that is more apt to undervalue those that are versed only in other parts of knowledge, than many of our modern naturalists."[1] He exposes their narrow-mindedness: "They esteem nothing save the laws and phenomena of nature to be subjects worthy of a philosophical pen."[2] He shows up their arrogance in presuming to speak on behalf of *the* scientific world: "It has long been the custom of such men to talk as if they were not just the best, but almost the only naturalists."[3]

Boyle notes that because of their pride they are not open to arguments in favor of religion if these arguments come "from professed divines."[4] In those cases, moreover, they accuse the clergy of self-interest.[5] In short, "he is the fittest to commend divinity whose profession it is not."[6] Since "it is notorious that in the age we live in" many people are likely to be more impressed by the arguments of a layman, especially of "a not undiligent cultivator of experimental philosophy [like Boyle himself]," therefore Boyle sees fit, in his arguments and illustrations, "both to employ comparisons drawn from telescopes, microscopes, etc., and to make frequent use of the [newer] notions, hypotheses and observations," for such a procedure is "either more clear, or . . . wont to be more acceptable than any other to our modern virtuosi."[7]

Given this situation, who, Boyle wonders, will stand up to them and come to the defense of religion? Divines are commonly too unacquainted with nature to manage it, and naturalists commonly esteem it no part of their work.[8] Therefore Boyle feels a strong

---

[1] *The Excellency of Theology;* 4:3.

[2] *The Christian Virtuoso;* 5:510.

[3] *The Usefulness of Natural Philosophy;* 2:59.

[4] *The Christian Virtuoso;* 5:509.

[5] *The Style of Holy Scripture;* 2:249.

[6] *The Excellency of Theology;* 4:2. [Cf. *Life;* 1:lx: " . . . the less he shares in the patrimony of the church."]

[7] *The Christian Virtuoso;* 5:509.

[8] *The Usefulness of Natural Philosophy;* 2:62.

compulsion to take up the pen himself,[1] not only to defend religion against the natural philosophers but also to come to the defense of the study of nature against timid Christians. He has to contend with investigators of nature who bring science into disrepute by coupling atheism to it, and with a certain class of theologians who bring theology into disrepute by opposing scientific research.

Boyle testifies emphatically that the study of nature has not led him to deny the Creator or his providence, nor to disesteem his Word, that "grand instrument of conveying to us the truths and mysteries of the Christian religion."[2] Thus he denies not only that the study of nature leads to atheism but also that it leads to deism, a natural religion without special revelation. The purpose of his last great work, *The Christian Virtuoso,* is to show, in the words of the subtitle: "that by being addicted to Experimental Philosophy, a man is rather assisted than indisposed to be a good Christian."[3]

Boyle is conscious that he is one of the foremost natural scientists of his day and at the same time that the Christian religion governs his life. Nevertheless he realizes that this will not move a bigoted adversary to truly listen. He complains that it is not uncommon among scientists to look down somewhat upon theology: "a man must have very great abilities otherwise, to make amends for the disadvantage of valuing sacred studies." His theological interests are viewed as a weakness in Mr. Boyle, who is said to be a learned and witty man of science *in spite of* his religious convictions.[4]

That is the usual response. Boyle's theology is considered a weakness in a man who is so intelligent otherwise. Some of his contemporaries decided they would just have to blame it on his melancholia.

---

[1] That his circle shared this feeling is evident from a letter by Edward Stillingfleet of 6 Oct. 1662, in which he urges Boyle to publish his work in behalf of the Christian religion and against Hobbes, in order that everyone might see that someone who is so intimately acquainted with nature nevertheless does not scorn religion: "I could heartily wish you would please to communicate to the world those papers . . . in behalf of Christianity (against Hobbes), that it may be seen yet further, that those great personages, who have courted nature so highly that her cabinets are open to them, are far from looking on religion as mean and contemptible." *Letters;* 6:462.

[2] *The Style of Holy Scripture;* 2:253.

[3] *The Christian Virtuoso;* 5:508.

[4] Cf. *The Excellency of Theology;* 4:2–5.

But others fared no better. In the case of Pascal, his mental equilibrium is said to have been disturbed; Newton, we are told, was for a time abnormal and was mentally deteriorating when he occupied himself with theology.[1] In short, once certain nineteenth-century historians got it into their heads that a shrewd scientist could hardly be a Christian they could only extricate themselves from an impasse by ascribing to their hero some mental disorder. And whenever religion plays a more limited role in the work of a scientist while its acknowledgment is not lacking (as in Gassendi and Galileo), he is depicted as a clever dissimulator who hoodwinks the clergy by a formal bow to the altar. This explains in part why so little attention has been paid to Boyle's physico-theological labours: those, supposedly, were a nonessential appendix to his works.[2] But whoever is of that opinion must pretend he is deaf when he hears Boyle say that he "had rather any of his papers passed by unperused" than those parts that treat of theological subjects.[3]

In Boyle's view, the danger posed to the Christian by the study of nature is grossly exaggerated. People allow themselves to be tricked by the clamor of the atheists into believing that *they* are the true cultivators of science, but Boyle shows that there is much affectation among them—that they flirt with their libertinism and their atheism: they are men who "would pass for virtuosi [yet] have but superficial (though conspicuous) wits [and] are not fitted to penetrate such truths as require a lasting and attentive speculation," while others among them, though not wanting in abilities, "are so taken up by their secular affairs and their sensual pleasures that they neither have the disposition nor the leisure to discover those truths that require both an attentive and penetrating mind."[4] Their irreligion, according to Boyle, is based on bias: it was not the study of nature that led them to irreligion; they

---

[1] On the falsehood of these views, see H. J. E. Beth, *Newton's Principia,* pt. II, pp. 136–38.

[2] This standpoint may perhaps be understandable in someone who personally attaches no value to religion, but it is far less excusable in some of Boyle's co-religionists who have ignored this aspect of his work. From them one might expect a serious interest in and study of the history of science; cf. my *Natuurwetenschap en Religie in het licht der historie*, address for the nineteenth academic meeting of the Free University on 4 July 1934; pub. in Assen, 1934, p. 28. More has been done in this area by Roman Catholics, e.g. Pierre Duhem, who showed that the "Dark Ages" are a fairy tale.

[3] *The Usefulness of Natural Philosophy;* 2:62.

[4] *The Christian Virtuoso;* 5:509.

carried it into their science and wanted to confirm it there.[1] They are blinded by self-interest, prejudice, passions, appetite.[2] We must not forget that Boyle had to contend not only with so-called philosophical atheists but also with shallow rakes from London[3] who covered their lack of morals with a cloak of philosophy. He entertained little hope that he might convert such people: "if the knowledge of nature falls into the hands of a resolved atheist, or a sensual libertine, he may misemploy it to impugn the grounds, or discredit the practice, of religion."[4]

Boyle knew that such people often admired science only from a distance. Naturally, to their hedonistic atheism painstaking research appeared much less attractive than their own pseudo-philosophical arguments, supported by scientific data whose import they could not appreciate. It is Boyle's expectation, however, that a personal investigation of nature cannot but lead a "man of probity and ingenuity, or at least free from prejudices and vices," to sentiments of religion.[5] He is of the opinion that the experimental study of nature disposes the mind to look for deeper-lying causes and thus prepares a person to seek after God. The libertines of today say with Pilate, What is truth? but they do not stay for an answer, for they have no time for the study of truths that require serious application; they are "a sort of superficial and desultory wits" who cannot be bothered to reflect upon the existence of God. But he who is accustomed to intricate and laborious experimentation will not easily be deterred from prosecuting the discovery of truths.[6]

Thus at bottom the issue, as Boyle sees it, is that most libertines, although they talk a lot about experimental science, do not themselves engage in it. Sometimes they did: for it was a fad among London's "high life" to dabble in experiments; king Charles II, a dilettant in this field as well, gave the example.[7] But this sort of engagement in science

---

[1] Ibidem; 514.

[2] Ibidem; 510.

[3] "This libertine city." Ibidem; 515.

[4] Ibidem; 514.

[5] Ibidem.

[6] Ibidem; 523f.

[7] Cf. Pepys, *Diary,* 30 May 1667. Macaulay, *History of England,* 1:401f, writes: "It was almost necessary to the character of a fine gentleman to have something to say about airpumps and telescopes; and even fine ladies, now and then, thought it becoming to affect a taste for science . . . ." Of course this was not true of everyone. The first president of the Royal Society, Lord

was superficial and biased. "If any of the cultivators of real [experimental] philosophy pervert it to countenance atheism, it is certainly the fault of the persons, not the doctrine, which is to be judged of by its own natural tendency, not by the ill use that some bad men may make of it."[1] Moreover, most if not all philosophers of this sort are but "pretenders" to the philosophy they misuse: "most of these do as little *understand* the mysteries of nature as *believe* those of Christianity."[2]

Coming from an otherwise mild-tempered man like Boyle, this judgment sounds harsh. In his eyes, they are very nearly always second-rate minds who press science into the service of their anti-religion. We cannot help but think here of men like Holbach, La Mettrie, Buechner and Haeckel, who surely cannot be put on a par with Kepler, Pascal, Boyle, Newton and Faraday! Just as in Boyle's days the believers allowed themselves to be scared away by the ranting of the self-styled "spokesmen of science," so in the 19th century simple Christians acquired a holy fear of that study that was so "dangerous" to the faith. The arrogant, apodictic tone of the Buechners, of course, sounded very imposing to the layperson.

And yet in 1660 it had "long been the custom of such men to talk as if they were not just the best, but almost the only naturalists"![3] But Boyle's position was strong; his circle, the Royal Society, which practiced experimental instead of speculative science, counted among its members all the important mathematicians and natural scientists of his day, and these were men who were confirmed Christians: Wren, Wallis, Ward, Newton, etc. It was precisely the man who in Boyle's eyes was so extremely dangerous and impious, Hobbes, who upbraided the Royal Society for its experimenting and declared it fruitless unless it rested on the foundation of *his* philosophy. Boyle sees very clearly that his opponents confuse their philosophical systems—the atomistic, which was often infected with atheism; the Cartesian and the peripatetic, which were not free of deistic bias—with the experimental philosophy grounded in experience.

From the side of religion it is objected that science is unsafe for the Christian because it explains everything from secondary causes and therefore thinks it can dispense with the primary cause, God. This

---

William Brouncker, was an able physician and mathematician. Samuel Pepys (1633–1703), commissioner of the navy, elected president in 1684, was an interested and modest amateur.

[1] *The Christian Virtuoso;* 5:514.

[2] Ibidem (emphasis added).

[3] *The Usefulness of Natural Philosophy;* 2:59.

objection is not shared by Boyle, for if he fails to mention God as cause in his scientific investigations, that is not because he sees no occasion for it but because he believes it is a wrong method for science to invoke non-physical causes. If it were indeed the case that science makes God a superfluous concept, I would counsel against it, says Boyle, "for I had much rather have men not philosophers than not Christians."[1] The objection is valid only, he concedes, in the case of superficial investigators, for whoever stops to think long enough knows that secondary causes do not by far explain everything, nor can they, so that one cannot but arrive at the primary cause. As his highest authority for this view Boyle quotes his revered Bacon, "who scruples not to affirm 'that a little or superficial taste of natural philosophy may, perchance, incline the mind of a man to atheism; but a full draught thereof brings the mind back again to religion . . . '"[2]; at first one cleaves to the secondary causes, but no sooner does one perceive the deeper causes and their interconnections than one discovers that the "highest link of nature's chain must needs be tied to the foot of Jupiter's chair."[3]

Boyle translates the point into somewhat more biblical language, with an allusion to Genesis 28: science affords us a ladder whose top reaches to the footstool of God's throne.[4] He goes on to quote Bacon with approval where he writes:

> No man should think that a man can search too far, or be too well studied, in the book of God's word, or in the book of God's works, in divinity or philosophy. But rather let men awake themselves, and cheerfully endeavour and pursue an endless progress or proficiency in both.[5]

Boyle agrees. Progress is to be endless. He is not yet ready for the pessimism instilled in some people precisely because of the endlessness of that progress!

---

[1] Ibidem; 15.

[2] Even Plato already remarks in the *Laws* that the timorous warn against astronomical and mathematical studies because they breed atheism. This is true, however, only of superficial study; serious investigation is a religious duty. Cf. Constanz Ritter, *Platon, sein Leben, seine Schriften, seine Lehre* (Munich, 1923), 2:413. See also Plato's *Timaios,* 90c, 90d.

[3] Francis Bacon, *The Advancement of Learning,* Book I.

[4] *The Usefulness of Natural Philosophy;* 2:58.

[5] Ibidem.

The only danger that the study of nature poses, Boyle thinks, is that we may become preoccupied with it, so that we neglect its chief end, which is to know God. Thus the danger is more a matter of lingering over the creatures than of actually denying God.[1]

§ 2. God's Revelation in Nature

a. Natural Theology
The general opinion of theologians, both Reformed and Roman Catholic, has always been that Nature is one of the means by which God reveals himself. Boyle too subscribes whole-heartedly to this conviction: "Such a care has God taken to make his being conspicuous in his creatures, that they all seem to speak loudly and unanimously: 'Know ye, that the LORD he is God; it is he that hath made us.'"[2] Almost all writers on natural theology are agreed that the universe teaches "both that there is a God, and that he is the author of it."[3] Boyle is sure that an honest study of nature must convince even the atheist (though it may not convert him).[4] Approvingly he quotes Bacon's observation that God never wrought a miracle to convince atheists, "because in his visible works He has placed enough to do it."[5]

Boyle believes that even those who are deprived of the Christian revelation can yet arrive at a natural religion through the study of nature.[6]

---

[1] *The Usefulness of Natural Philosophy*; 2:60.

[2] Ibidem; 56, quoting Ps. 100:3.

[3] Ibidem; 35.

[4] *The Christian Virtuoso;* 5:510.

[5] Ibidem; 514.

[6] We have already pointed out that for Boyle this "natural theology" too is a *revelation* of God. In the case of natural revelation, as in the case of Scripture, man is bound to a *given* which he has certainly not conceived on his own, nor would have conceived in this way—in other words, which is not rational to the bottom. This circumstance defines the difference between, on the one hand, a natural theology that is built on God's revelation in nature and on a "spark" left to every man by God's common grace, and, on the other hand, a natural theology that is purely rational, which is to say, one that is entirely based on metaphysical reflection. The latter kind is certainly not the natural knowledge of God meant by St. Paul, although the apostle does mean a general revelation of God apart from special revelation: "God left not himself without witness" (Acts 14:17), not even to the heathens that know not the Scriptures.

[T]he universal experience of all ages manifests, that the contemplation of the world has been much more prevalent to make those,
that have addicted themselves to it, believers, than deniers of a
Deity. For it is very apparent that the old philosophers, for the
most part, acknowledged a God; and [just] as evident it is, by their
want of revelation, by many passages in their writings, and by
divers other things . . . that the consideration of the works of
nature was the chief thing that induced them to acknowledge a
divine author of them.[1]

This view Boyle finds supported in Scripture: "St. Paul seems to
inform us (Rom. 1:20) that the invisible things of God are clearly seen
from the creation of the world," so that the gentiles, who had but the
light of nature, are without excuse and might come to a knowledge of
the true God.[2] Thus Boyle sees confirmed in historical experience and
Scripture alike what personal experience had taught him.[3]

The study of the universe, Boyle maintains, so far from tempting
the observer to ascribe its excellencies to "so incompetent and pitiful
a cause as blind chance, or the tumultuous justlings of atomical portions
of senseless matter," will lead him instead to the acknowledgment and

---

[1] *The Usefulness of Natural Philosophy;* 2:55.

[2] Ibidem; 34f. *The Christian Virtuoso;* 5:514.

[3] To defend Boyle on this point would be needless, were it not for certain
groups of theologians of various persuasions who like to call themselves
"Calvinists" and who reject natural theology with an appeal to Calvin. This is
the effect of that passion for system which Boyle condemns so strongly in
theologians (and in Descartes); they desire a coherent system and therefore do
violence to reality. Hence Boyle says that non-theologians sometimes read and
explicate Scripture more simply and faithfully than the theologians, who are
biased because they desire only to draw their system from it. Indeed, they lift
a certain aspect out of the Bible (or out of Calvin) and look at it through a
magnifying glass, producing a distorted picture of the whole. To reject a
natural knowledge of God, however, is to be diametrically opposed to Scripture
(Rom. 1:20; Acts 14:17), to the Belgic Confession (Art. 2), and to Calvin
himself, who sharply condemns a neglecting of natural theology: to reject it is
contrary to experience, is irreligious, shows ingratitude, and contradicts God's
Word; see G. Gloede, *Theologia naturalis bei Calvin* (Stuttgart, 1935). Writes
E. Choisy, *Calvin et la science* (Geneva, 1931), p. 12: "to neglect his teaching
concerning common grace and general revelation is to ignore an important
facet of his genius, is to condemn oneself to miss the grandeur of his mind."
See also my *Natuurwetenschap en Religie in het licht der historie,* pp. 10f.
[Idem, *Religion and the Rise of Modern Science* (Edinburgh and London, 1972)
chap. v.]

adoration of "a most intelligent, powerful, and benign Author of
things." The believer will find that knowledge of the creation confirms
his faith in the Creator. "I am persuaded," Boyle writes, "that nature
will be found very loyal to her Author," and that the motives for
embracing religion are "highly rational and just."[1] There is no question
for Boyle of any *threat* to religion from the study of nature: but that is
not the most important issue for him in any case. The argument which
to his mind is decisive is that the study of nature is our *duty!* If this
holds even for the ancient pagans, who had only natural revelation and
the innate principles of moral virtues,[2] how much more for the
Christian, who accepts Scripture as God's revelation: Scripture enjoins
the study of nature as a sacred obligation; God intended that his
creatures not only supply the needs of our animal part but also give
instructions to our intellectual part.[3] God loves to be honored in *all* our
faculties and, consequently, "to be glorified and acknowledged by the
acts of reason as well as by those of faith."[4]

Boyle does not consider it presumptuous to suppose that in
creating the world one of God's principal ends was to manifest his own
glory,[5] and since in the age-old controversy whether the understanding
or the will is primary in man he has the rationalistic inclination to grant
priority to the understanding, it follows that he considers an intellectual
knowledge of God, acquired through the study of nature, of eminent
importance: whoever would deter men from the scrutiny of nature tends
to "defeat God of much of that glory which man both ought and might
ascribe to him."[6]

Now it is commonly seen, no less in our day, that half-science
and religion are mutual enemies, whereas a really thorough engagement
in science restores in men a humble attitude with respect to religion
because they realize science cannot answer the deepest questions. Bacon
and Boyle assert repeatedly that only half-knowledge leads away from
God. But what intrigues us at this moment is the question of what
Boyle thinks of a naive knowledge of nature. Given his intellectualistic
bent, the answer is not hard to guess.

On Boyle's view, we must not halt at a superficial contemplation
and admiration of God's work in nature; it is our duty, as far as

---

[1] *The Christian Virtuoso;* 5:514.
[2] *The Excellency of Theology;* 4:28.
[3] *The Usefulness of Natural Philosophy;* 2:19.
[4] Ibidem; 31.
[5] Ibidem; 15.
[6] Ibidem; 30.

possible, in a clear and rational way, to ascertain the attributes of God from the creatures, which are as it were made for that purpose. A peasant admires the rich enamel on the case of his watch; a craftsman's admiration goes much deeper, as he appreciates the inner workings of the watch.[1] God has not displayed all that workmanship in the world in order that we should wilfully close our eyes to it. The study of the universe is "the first act of religion, and equally obliging in all religions: it is the duty of man as man, and the homage we pay for the privilege of reason."[2]

Boyle demands of man a "philosophical worship." For "an active and operative intuition" of God's perfections excites an admiration, "with the devotion springing thence," that will be so much the more intensive as it is the "more rational."[3]

With youthful enthusiasm[4] Boyle speaks about this philosophical worship in a lyrical effusion that we seldom meet in him. He writes:

> . . . the sublimest knowledge here attainable will not destroy, but only heighten and ennoble our admiration, and will prove the incense or more spiritual and acceptable part of that sacrifice of praise . . . wherein the intelligent admirer offers the whole world in eucharists to its Maker. For admiration (I do not say astonishment or surprise) being an acknowledgement of the object's transcending our knowledge, the more learned the transcendent faculty is, the greater is the admired object's transcendency acknowledged. And certainly, God's wisdom is much less glorified by the vulgar astonishment of an unlettered starer (whose ignorance may be as well suspected for his wonder, as the excellency of the object) than from their learned hymns, whose industrious curiosity hath brought their understandings to a prostrate veneration of what their reason, not ignorance, hath taught them not to be perfectly comprehensible by them.
>
> And as such persons have such piercing eyes, that where a transient or unlearned glance scarce observes anything, they can discern an adorable wisdom, being able (as I may so speak) to read the stenography of God's omniscient hand; so their skilful fingers know how to choose and how to touch those strings that may sound

---

[1] Ibidem.

[2] Ibidem; 62.

[3] Ibidem.

[4] The tract *Some Considerations Touching the Usefulness of Experimental Natural Philosophy* came out in 1663; the first five chapters, however, had been written a good ten years earlier, thus when Boyle was only about 22 years old (cf. preface, 2:3f).

sweetest to the praise of their Maker. . . . [A]s God hath not, by becoming our Saviour, laid by his first relation to us as our Creator, . . . so neither hath he given up his right to those intelligent adorations from us, which become us on account of being his rational creatures; neither are such performances made less acceptable to him by the filial relation into which Christ hath brought us to him . . . And the Scripture mentions as a very acceptable part of religious worship the 'sacrifice of praise, and the calves of our lips'; by offering up of which we make that true use of the creatures, of so referring them to their Creator's glory that . . . as 'all things are of him, and through him,' so they may be 'to him; to whom be glory for ever. Amen.'[1]

Boyle is persuaded that "rational, reasonable worship" in the study of nature solemnizes God's praise as much as does choral music in the worship service. For such reflections, which by their nature are mere "acts of reason," may by their *end* be made "acts of piety."[2]

And so as a Christian scientist Boyle has the proud sense of being a priest of natural religion. It makes him angry sometimes to meet with those who cannot worship God except as Protestants or Catholics and never come to worship Him as humans; he is offended by those who neglect the "philosophical worship of God."[3]

b. Teleological Proofs of God the Creator

Natural religion covers a wider terrain than just divine revelation in nature. One may accept the latter and reject the former, namely when one thinks that only he who is already a believer will find God in Nature. Inversely, one may deny divine revelation in nature and yet acknowledge natural religion (as did Descartes). Natural religion, after all, comprises not only the religion that one acquires through contemplating nature but also every form of religious knowledge that bypasses any "special" revelation and is accessible to everyone through contemplation and reflective thought. Thus according to Boyle the mere

---

[1] *The Usefulness of Natural Philosophy;* 2:63, quoting Heb. 13:15 and Rom. 11:36.
[2] Ibidem.
[3] Ibidem; 62f.

consideration of the human mind and its innate notions[1] points to the existence of a Deity.[2]

Not surprisingly, Boyle derives his arguments for natural theology especially from experimental philosophy: the latter leads to a firm belief in the existence of God, "which belief is, in the order of things, the first principle of that natural religion which itself is pre-required to revealed religion in general."[3] He must maintain this against those who for whatever reason do not wish to construct a natural theology through the study of nature (Descartes among others), but above all against the Epicureans, who think the world arose by chance.

His most important argument for the first article of natural religion is creation's purposeful design, thus the teleological proof of God. From an intelligent Maker it is to be expected that what He does has a purpose; thus the elimination of chance and the demonstration of final causes converge for Boyle in the certainty of the existence of God the Creator. This proof is elaborated by him particularly in *A Disquisition About the Final Causes of Natural Things.* He makes the usual distinction between efficient causes, which indicate *how* phenomena arise, and final causes, which indicate *why* things are the way they are.

The more or less mechanically operating efficient causes still leave some room for the possibility that "chance" or blind determinism alone is the cause of the phenomena; but if Boyle can show that there are final causes at work in nature it is established for him beyond denial that there is an intelligent cause. That is not to say that efficient causes have meaning for him only in science and not in theology: they ascend ever higher, after all, and thus lead to the Cause of all causes; they point to a creative *force.* This is the meaning of Boyle's remark that

---

[1] Sometimes Boyle hesitates between the view that the mind has "innate ideas" and the view that nothing is in the mind that was not first in the senses. The latter (sensualist) standpoint is represented especially by John Locke, whose active career, however, came later (after 1689). In general, Boyle has greater sympathy for the first-mentioned standpoint, which is also that of his friends, the Cambridge Platonists (Cudworth and his associates), who go so far as to repudiate all forms of sensualism. In any event, he does not attach too much importance to those "innate ideas"; see below, chap. IV, sec. 2c.

Boyle and Locke had a good relationship; they shared an interest in natural research (in which Locke did not accomplish all that much) and both worked assiduously for religious toleration.

The doctrine of sensualism, which at first seemed rather suspect, was incorporated in the arguments of both deists and apologists in the 18th century!

[2] *The Usefulness of Natural Philosophy;* 2:58. *The Christian Virtuoso;* 5:530.

[3] *The Christian Virtuoso;* 5:515.

"science affords us a ladder whose top reaches to the footstool of God's throne." But final causes show a well-laid *plan;* they therefore point much more directly to a creative *intelligence.*

Boyle's arguments against chance are worth noting. If Epicurus supposes that "this exquisite and stupendous fabrick of the world" is constituted by the fortuitous concourse of atoms, then Boyle objects that this is as improbable as that a multitude of small letters in a printer's shop, being thrown upon the ground, should fall into such an order as to exhibit the history of the creation of the world as described in the first four chapters of Genesis.[1] Thus he appeals to the infinitesimally low probability that such a highly organized architecture of atoms as nature affords could arise by chance.

This argument must have made a hit with the Epicureans of his day, for when it could be turned *against* religion they used it themselves. Boyle relates that according to them a dead body does not come back to life because of the high improbability that all the atoms will reassemble with their selfsame motions. This argument he now turns on them by dismissing the notion that man and animal, in short the entire purposeful universe, might arise by chance from atoms and motion.[2]

Boyle perceives that the more complicated a thing is, the less likely and therefore also the less contingent it is—and also, the more we are compelled to conjecture a rational guidance behind it. For this reason he prefers to draw his examples from the plant and animal kingdoms—in particular, from anatomy—and to a far lesser degree from inorganic nature. Proofs drawn from stones and metals he considers not very cogent[3]; nor do arguments from astronomy satisfy him: a human muscle is for him a more wonderful contrivance than the celestial orbs, and the eye of the common house-fly is a finer piece of workmanship than the body of the sun.[4] As for stones and metals (even a "silver plant," a crystalline aggregate), he might be able to imagine that they arose from "various occursions and justlings" of atoms: they are simple structures that do not particularly suggest the guidance of an intelligent cause; they are effects that follow from causes few in number and easy to reproduce. As for the origin of animals, however, so many causes have to work together harmoniously, and such a continued series of motions and operations is required, that it is utterly

---

[1] *The Usefulness of Natural Philosophy;* 2:43.

[2] Ibidem; 48.

[3] *Final Causes;* 5:403, 409f.

[4] Ibidem; 403.

inconceivable that they arose "without the superintendency of a rational Agent." The parts of a human body are complicated beyond compare to the simple texture of a crystalline substance.[1] In Boyle's eyes, the meanest limb of the body surpasses in artfulness the structure of the clock at Strassburg that he admired so much.[2] But the high point of art and design he finds in the eye. It is one of his favorite illustrations and he explains at length how the eyes of different animals serve specific purposes.[3] Although like Descartes he views animals as machines, animal *life* provides him with proof that they are nevertheless machines that serve an end; he draws his illustrations especially from the habits of bees, ants and spiders and from the curious structure of their respective nests.[4]

It is striking that also in later times the teleological view always got the most support from biologists; physicists and chemists, who explore the simple and "mechanical" laws of inorganic nature, have always been more inclined to embrace the mechanico-causal mode of explanation. Despite his pronounced preference for chemistry, Boyle was saved by his great interest in anatomy from basing his view of nature exclusively on inanimate nature.

Boyle does not want to press the argument from design as far as was often done, and although religiously speaking he regarded man as the center of creation,[5] he particularly does not want to argue too anthropocentrically. The sun is useful to man, but he cannot tell whether such is its sole or chief end.[6] He cannot see any use for us in fixed stars and solar eclipses.[7] However, we should not deem ourselves too important, as though everything has to be appreciated in terms of *our* immediate needs.[8] We do not see, or not yet see, the usefulness of many things: not until the recent discovery by "our famous Harvey" has the usefulness of valves in the veins become apparent.[9] For that matter, to perceive the final causes is not always easy, for it is not unusual "that a thing more excellent [is] employed for the good of one that is less so," or, equally, that the interest of the lesser is subordi-

---

[1] Ibidem.
[2] Ibidem; 404.
[3] Ibidem; 405–8.
[4] Ibidem; 424–32. *The Usefulness of Natural Philosophy;* 2:23.
[5] *Final Causes;* 5:412.
[6] Ibidem; 403, 411.
[7] Ibidem; 416, 424.
[8] Ibidem; 417.
[9] Ibidem; 427.

nated to the greater: what is hurtful to one individual may be beneficial to the whole nation.[1]

Ultimately, in all these things it is the spiritual factor that predominates for Boyle. Although in physical respects man is a tiny and negligible part of the universe, he alone has a rational soul; he alone therefore can know and serve God and outshine the largest heavenly body, which has no soul.[2] And that is why Boyle is also of the opinion that the astronomical spaces—the distance of the stars and the immensity of the heavens—, which are of little use to us as human beings, are nevertheless, albeit not physically, yet spiritually useful because they cause us to admire God's infinite greatness.[3]

And so we see Boyle uphold, if perhaps not as powerfully as a Pascal, the Christian view: man's humble state as he stands before mighty nature, and on the other hand, man's pride in being the only one in nature who knows that he exists and who is able with his mind to explore this great universe, which does not even know that it exists.

In defending final causes Boyle opposes Epicurus, because he thinks they do not exist,[4] and Descartes, because he says they cannot be discovered. Aristotle, who does accept final causes, is of no help to him, because he acknowledges them on false grounds. Thus Boyle finds support only among physicians and anatomists, who like himself build on observations rather than reason.

It must not be supposed that Descartes would have any objection to natural theology; a "rational" proof of God fits in perfectly with his conception. But Descartes' natural theology bears a much more rationalistic stamp than Boyle's, which rests on empirical research.

Descartes, then, deems it presumptuous to think that human reason might discover what ends God had in mind at creation, since they are too exalted for that.[5] If it seems odd that the founder of rationalism is so humble in the face of the Divine Reason, we need only remember that he was afraid of the teleological and anthropocentric arguments of scholasticism, which were indeed an *asylum ignorantiae.*[6] Boyle shares Descartes' aversion to them, but when Descartes

---

[1] *Final Causes*; 5:412, 417.

[2] Ibidem; 415f.

[3] Ibidem; 416.

[4] In combating the errors of the Epicureans, he expressly makes an exception for Gassendi. Ibidem; 393.

[5] Cartesius, *Principia Philosophiae,* pt I, art. 28.

[6] *Final Causes;* 5:395.

jettisons the search for final causes *altogether* with a pious argument, Boyle shows that Descartes is a fox who does himself what he attacks in others.

For consider: Descartes postulates that the quantity of motion is constant because God is immutable and therefore preserves what he gave in the beginning. But that, Boyle comments justly, is just as much a judgment about God's design, and a far worse one. He (Boyle) wishes merely to infer *a posteriori* what God was pleased to choose from the many possibilities open to him, whereas Descartes emphatically states *a priori* what God cannot do. So if the issue is "not to judge of God's designs," Descartes has struck a blow at himself more than at a teleologian of the type of Boyle. With Descartes, God's design is limited to one knowable to us: but why might God not be able to accomplish his design best by "sometimes adding to, and sometimes taking from, the quantity of motion?"[1] This question of Boyle's is all the more compelling since Descartes has not established *experimentally* that the quantity of motion is constant!

Boyle also turns the tables on Descartes' other argument against final causes, namely that one should assume only physical causes: Descartes himself assumes non-physical foundations for his system when he reasons that since motion does not belong to the essence of matter, matter must owe the motion it has to some other, immaterial being, *viz.* God. As well, his assertion that the quantity of motion in the universe is constant *because God is immutable* is clearly a *meta-physical* argument.[2]

For the rest, Boyle is no less than Descartes inclined to banish all immaterial agents and all final causes from *physical* explanation. His purely experimental works,[3] consequently, have no references to final causes.[4] But apart from being an experimental physicist he is also a natural philosopher; he *has* to be, the moment he begins to reflect upon the value and significance of the knowledge acquired, and the moment he reasons backwards from secondary to primary causes. He cannot artificially close himself off to the deeper-lying questions; he is compelled to move from the how to the why of things, to end up,

---

[1] Ibidem; 396.

[2] Ibidem; 399.

[3] *The Sceptical Chymist; New Experiments Touching the Spring and Weight of the Air,* etc.

[4] From his earliest works he avoided such references: "me, who in physical inquiries of this nature look for efficient rather than final causes." *Against Linus;* 1:143.

finally, at theology. Boyle's great merit, however, is that *methodologically* he separates the purely scientific part of his work, both experiments and hypotheses, from the philosophical and theological parts.

Boyle is not someone who for the sake of the "higher" final causes forgets about the "lower" efficient causes; he does not belong to those sublime minds who, quietly philosophizing from their armchairs, think they see more deeply than the plodders in the laboratories. No, respect for the material world, which is just as much a creation of God, is too deeply entrenched in him.[1] In Boyle, the separation of science and philosophy is a division of labor. The search for final causes, he writes, "is not the proper task of the naturalist, whose work, as he is such, is not so much to discover why, as how, particular effects are produced. . . . [The aims] of physics are, to understand *how* nature produces the phenomenon we contemplate; and, in case it be imitable by us, how we may, if occasion require, produce the like effect."[2]

But neither does Boyle belong to the perhaps clever but also restricted minds who wish to exhaust science in technique. He knows that the true investigator of nature at last takes stock of his knowledge and cannot help but look at his results within a larger framework. That is still true today, witness the many "philosophizing" works of well-known physicists and astronomers like Planck, Jordan, Jeans and Eddington. Boyle, then, believes that, for all our acknowledgment of the efficient causes, we may also view nature from the other side now and then, especially when the issue concerns the general causes of the world and not the course of nature as already established,[3]—in other words, especially when we move beyond experimentation. A watch may be accounted for by its mechanism, but also by the end for which the watchmaker designed it.[4] The clock at Strassburg is no "casual concurrence": that it has precisely those measurements is proper to its design.[5] Similarly, a quill, dipped in ink and moved across white paper—"all which are corporeal things" explainable from mechanical causes—may very well trace a rational discourse, but "would never

---

[1] As it is in all those, for that matter, who to a greater or lesser degree hold the Reformed worldview.

[2] *Final Causes;* 5:443.

[3] Ibidem; 399.

[4] Ibidem.

[5] *The Usefulness of Natural Philosophy;* 2:48.

have been moved after the requisite manner upon the paper, had not its motion been guided and regulated by the understanding of the writer."[1]

Boyle has a keen insight into the difference between the approach of the philosopher and the physicist. He has not the slightest intention to reduce the human mind (which embraces the universe, after all!) to a part of the human body, hence to an infinitessimally small part of the universe. It does not occur to him either, therefore, thoughtlessly to assimilate that mind into the mechanical clockwork. His example of human writing is a pithy way of saying that the causality of the mind is different from that of matter. Much fruitless debate about determinism might have been prevented by this distinction. Reality would probably not have been explained any better, but it would have been accepted more easily. For that is what Boyle, for all his rationalism, ultimately does!

If nature is declared to "produce things in a way that is most agreeable to our reason," he replies: "What we are to inquire after is how things are really produced, not whether or no the manner of their production be such as may the most easily be understood by us." God's knowledge infinitely transcends ours; he may be supposed to operate according to the dictates of his own immense wisdom, so why should he have respect to "the measure and ease of human understandings?"[2] This is another blow at the Cartesians, who base their whole system precisely on the human understanding. In a sense, they generate the world through their rational deductions in the same way as the rational Creator called it forth in actuality. So if the issue is not to overestimate human reason and to avoid arrogant presumption, certainly no charge will lie with Boyle, who simply wants to ascertain by means of the senses and the intellect how creation operates, even though it turns out only in part to lie within the grasp of reason, for another part to lie far beyond reason's scope. Descartes may very piously refuse to infer the Divine final causes from *nature,* yet he derives the Divine efficient causes from human *reason!* Boyle seems to have sensed this remarkable contradiction: if Descartes has demonstrated the existence of God from an "innate idea which He left upon the mind of man as the mark of an artist impressed upon his work," then Boyle's comment is: "I see not why we may not reasonably think that God . . . may also have [done

---

[1] Ibidem.
[2] Ibidem; 46.

so] by stamping characters, or living impresses, as well without, upon the world, as within, upon the mind."[1]

At this point the contrast between rationalism and empiricism is transposed to the theological terrain. The contrast in fact extends even further. Descartes is eager to have an intelligible world; Boyle no less, and he does not neglect to praise the rationality of his science and of his religion in glowing terms. But experience forces him constantly to admit that much of the world is *not* intelligible. Even if this world were intelligible throughout, he says, the question still remains: Why *this* world?[2] And that brings us back to our starting point, namely Boyle's criticism of Descartes, who restricts God's design to a scheme knowable to us.[3]

There is yet another point on which Boyle criticizes Descartes, a purely theological one. Descartes states that we cannot know God's final causes if He himself does not *reveal* them to us (in a supernatural way) and that, although morally speaking it may be true for us humans that all things were made for the glory of God, thus obligating men to praise God for his works, metaphysically speaking "it is childish and absurd to think that God, like a proud man, would have no other purpose in constructing the world than to be praised of men, and that he made the sun, which is so much larger than the earth, for no other purpose than to afford light to man, who is but a small part of it." To this Boyle replies: Descartes cannot prove that God did *not* make, among other things, the world in order to be praised by us. Why would it be absurd that the great sun is made for man? "That most excellent engine of man's body is a more admirable thing than the sun, and the rational and immortal soul that resides in it is incomparably more noble than a thousand masses of brute matter."[4] Thus *on this question* Boyle will not be confined to scientific arguments; here he defies Descartes by defending the glory of the human mind, because Descartes, who otherwise boasts of it, here uses the greatness of the material world to crush man.

But he also tackles Descartes for saying "if God does not reveal them to us." For Boyle has Bible texts aplenty to prove that God does. Then all science and philosophy yield to the authority of Scripture, for even if "the consideration of the things themselves did not give us the

---

[1] *Final Causes;* 5:401f.

[2] Cf. a similar remark in Kepler, who says somewhere that "a comparison of worlds makes no sense."

[3] *Final Causes;* 5:397.

[4] Ibidem; 400.

least suspicion" of God's purposes, "if the revelations contained in the holy scriptures be admitted, we may rationally believe more, and speak less hesitantly, of the ends of God than bare philosophy will warrant us to do."[1] In other words, Cartesians who accept the authority of Scripture are bound to accept final causes. However, although on Boyle's view Descartes tends to deprive us of "one of the best and most successful arguments to convince men that there is a God," nevertheless Boyle disavows the oft repeated accusation that Descartes consciously favors atheism.[2]

c. Proofs of God's Providence

The study of nature, according to Boyle, thus yields the most powerful arguments for the existence of God. But in addition it reveals to us the attributes of God: his power, wisdom and goodness. His power is manifest in his having brought forth the great universe out of nothing.[3] His wisdom is written with such large letters that even the ordinary reader can read them, how much more those who see deeper. The marvelous engine of the eye or muscle can be fully appreciated only by him who has mastered anatomy, mechanics, optics, mathematics, and also chemistry (because of the action of body fluids). An anatomist likewise "has much stronger invitations to believe" than someone who never witnessed a dissection.[4] Again and again Boyle illustrates his point with the clock at Strassburg: Whoever sees that machine, which now works according to the rules desired by its maker, cannot but come to admire that author. The human eye, however, is a much more wonderful machine; no *human* could contrive such an effective and ingenious piece of workmanship. It was an example that made all the more impression on Boyle's contemporaries because they shared his view that even animals are "nature's clocks" or "living engines"[5]; on the basis of Harvey's discovery of the circulation of blood Boyle even speaks of "hydraulico-pneumatical engines."[6]

God's goodness, finally, is evident from his sustenance of the animal world. This is evident especially to man, for everything has

---

[1] Ibidem; 411.

[2] Ibidem; 401.

[3] *The Usefulness of Natural Philosophy;* 2:20.

[4] Ibidem; 21, 51f; see also *The Christian Virtuoso,* 5:516f.

[5] *The Usefulness of Natural Philosophy;* 2:22f.

[6] The human body according to Boyle is a "matchless engine," the hand an "admirable engine." Ibidem; 22, 51; see also *The Notion of Nature;* 5:232.

been subjected to him as God's image-bearer.[1] The rainbow (again an illustration from nature!) most emphatically proclaims God's goodness. Thus for his self-communication God wants to use not only words but also things; the world declares the glory of God to our "intellectual ears." The world is a "visible word," just like the sacraments.[2] Accordingly, in addition to the first great principle of natural theology (that there is a God, who has created the world), the contemplation of nature likewise teaches us that this God sustains the world through his providence.[3] In this way the contemplation of nature, or natural reason, brings man to the fulfilment of the two great duties of natural religion: to adore God, and to show him gratitude for his works.[4]

Having defended God's existence and God's act of creation against the atheists, Boyle next defends God's continuous sustenance of creation against the objections of a particular group of deists.[5]

God's providence must be acknowledged especially by the Cartesians, Boyle insists, because, first of all, they assume that motion is not inherent in matter hence must first be "produced in it, and is still every moment continued and preserved immediately by God," and secondly, because they believe that the rational soul is an immaterial substance that is inserted each time into the human embryo by a "direct and particular intervention" of God.[6]

Now some deists say that all things are brought to pass by the "settled laws of nature." Boyle's response to this is that he looks upon a law as a moral, not a physical cause. An inanimate body does not "act in accordance with" a law[7]; its actions are produced "by a *real power,* not by laws," and he who produces such actions may regulate the exertion of his power by settled rules.[8] Boyle means to say, therefore, not only that everything in nature owes its existence to God, but also that there is nothing in the "nature" of things that sustains them "in and of themselves"; that just as a free act of God made them to be *so,* gave them *those* rules, so also a continuous act of God's will is

---

[1] *The Usefulness of Natural Philosophy;* 2:29.

[2] Ibidem.

[3] *The Christian Virtuoso;* 5:519.

[4] Ibidem; 520.

[5] He usually calls them "theists," later also "deists." The use of the term "theist" for those who acknowledge a personal God, Creator and Sustainer, dates from a later time.

[6] *The Christian Virtuoso;* 5:520.

[7] *The Notion of Nature;* 5:170.

[8] *The Christian Virtuoso;* 5:520f.

necessary to keep them so and to keep them operating according to those rules. This view is entirely in line with Boyle's defence of miracles and his critique of the concept of Nature.[1]

Boyle's critique of the concept "Nature" is new for his time.[2] He examines the various meanings that the word has and impugns especially that usage in which it functions as an empty concept supplanting the Deity. Men speak of nature as though it were a being: "Nature abhors a vacuum, Nature does nothing in vain, etc., etc.," yet all the time it is a product of *our* mind, a "notional thing."[3]

Boyle here takes aim particularly at Aristotle and the advocates of an *anima mundi* or world-soul.[4] Since the Renaissance there had been a revival of a pagan Aristotelianism in opposition to Christian scholasticism. It depicted Nature as a living being which occasionally departs capriciously from its own rules. This Boyle opposes; he believes that everything must be explained in terms of matter and the laws of motion (with the aid of God) and he rejects the notion that an intelligent Nature intervenes.[5]

As a principle of explanation the concept "Nature" is unnecessary; it adds nothing to what may be deduced from matter and motion.[6] Boyle even considers it directly harmful for science: a man does not fulfil his task as a naturalist by ascribing something to nature, but rather by deducing a phenomenon "by intelligible ways, from intelligible principles."[7] If we cannot always explain things from intelligible mechanical principles, we must not for that reason have recourse right away to "nature."[8] We do better in those instances to confess "that we

---

[1] Cf. *A Free Inquiry into the Vulgarly Received Notion of Nature,* written in 1666 and published in 1682; 5:158–254.

[2] *The Notion of Nature;* 5:159, 254.

[3] Ibidem; 164.

[4] *The Usefulness of Natural Philosophy;* 2:38, 43.

[5] *The Notion of Nature;* 5:162.

[6] Ibidem; 189.

[7] Ibidem; 249.

[8] Boyle is conscious of the danger of anthropomorphic interpretations of nature, such as substituting empty words ("abhorrency of a vacuum") for genuine explanations, and ascribing "inclinations" to inanimate bodies. *The Usefulness of Natural Philosophy;* 2:38. He, by contrast, wants to explain everything (short of man's intellect and will) from mechanical causes that operate (with the assistance of the Deity) according to certain rules. Things may *seem* to have knowledge and understanding, but in the clock at Strassburg it is not each wheel that possesses intelligence, but the artificer; each

are at a loss how they are performed, and that this ignorance proceeds
. . . from the natural imperfection of our understandings . . . "[1] Of
many things we can say little more than *that* they are *so,* not *why* they
are *so* (the shapes and sizes of animals, the number and location of the
stars). In such instances we can say little more than that it pleased the
Creator to make them so. But that answer does not pretend to give a
physical reason.[2]

But does Boyle's critique not also affect his own faith in God? It
would seem so, at first glance, for he is not willing to assign any
function in scientific explanation either to God or to Nature. When
Linus states that it is by Divine Omnipotence ("divinitus") that a given
quantity of matter "virtually" extends itself (a notion that Boyle finds
inconceivable), then he (Boyle) responds: "Our controversy is not about
what *God* can do, but about what can be done by *natural agents* . . .
In *ours* things are explicated by the ordinary course of nature, whereas
in the other [hypothesis] recourse must be had to miracles."[3] In fact,
Boyle wants to deduce from the rules given by God even any seeming
anomalies in the regular course of nature.[4]

Boyle certainly believes that God also upholds nature, but then
only by freely binding himself to the rules he himself gave it. Science
is to seek out these rules, then treat them as "givens" and explain the
phenomena through them, without resorting to God as cause the
moment it feels powerless to offer a purely physical explanation.
Otherwise everything becomes a miracle. In no way does Boyle deny
that God can "interpose" in the regular course of things, but then it is
indeed a miracle in the full sense of the word; and miracles have no
place in science.

Accordingly, Boyle perceives very clearly that harm is done, not
just to science but also to religion, when "miracles" are introduced
everywhere. He makes the remark that those who assume a world-soul
or intelligent beings for guiding the planets in their irregular courses
are introducing miracles everywhere, even as they dissolve the genuine
concept of miracle. That is worse, in his opinion, than what the

---

component part does its duty, without knowing the whole. Similarly, the world
machine does not itself have intelligence or purpose, but God. The self-
preservation and propagation of things, accordingly, does not happen through
some "nature," but through God. Ibidem; 38f.

[1] *The Notion of Nature;* 5:246.

[2] Ibidem; 165.

[3] *Against Linus;* 1:149; emphasis added.

[4] *The Notion of Nature;* 5:163f.

Epicureans do, who deny the miracles of Christ because they cannot be explained from matter and motion, in other words, because they are *miracles*.[1]

Thus he condemns the introduction of Nature on religious grounds, for it is a "semi-deity,"[2] a creature, of the human imagination at that, to which attributes are ascribed that belong only to God.[3] The doctrine of matter and motion is more god-fearing than that of Nature; Aristotle's opinions are "more unfriendly, not to say pernicious" to religion than those of "several other heathen philosophers."[4]

No less does he condemn the concept of Nature in the name of science. Boyle wants to invoke ordinary *physical* causes, and science is rendered impossible if the phenomena are governed by a capricious being. In short, the "vulgar notion of nature" is not only injurious to the glory of God but also "a great impediment to the solid and useful discovery of his works."[5]

It is not Boyle but his adversaries who confuse religion and science. They resort to an idol, Nature, whereas he considers God too holy to use him as a mask for his own ignorance. Boyle defends a strictly causal science against the idolators of nature who, seemingly enlightened, deny or exclude the Deity and assign a role to their own chimeras, to the detriment of science and religion alike. According to this biblically informed "Christian Virtuoso," the Scriptures never speak of "nature," the philosophers of little else.[6]

Moreover, the concept of nature is unclear, for no one knows exactly what is understood by it, or whether it is a material or an immaterial thing.[7] Boyle himself is willing to use the word only as a short form for all of created reality with its rules, as a popular term, where accuracy is not required.[8]

From the acknowledgment of final causes it is clear that Boyle's position is closer to Gassendi's than to that of Descartes. True, Gassendi rehabilitated the atomism of Epicurus; but he enriched its content and introduced corrections which made it much more acceptable

---

[1] Ibidem; 164.
[2] Ibidem.
[3] Ibidem; 191.
[4] Ibidem; 163. Epicurus included?
[5] Ibidem; 162.
[6] Ibidem; 191.
[7] Ibidem.
[8] Ibidem; 249.

to the Christian world. Gassendi rejected the notion that the whole world arose by chance from atoms on the basis of an age-old argument: the improbability of the *Iliad* emerging from a jumble of letters thrown on the ground. We have seen how Boyle uses the same argument; his tendency to draw his images from the Bible rather than the classics is the only reason why he chooses Genesis as an example.

Gassendi, then, like Boyle, is of the opinion that an orderly, highly organized system points to a thought in which it is conceived. It follows that he also acknowledges final causes: in plants and animals, as well as in crystals, he recognizes an ordering that points to the pursuit of a goal or end which is attained through "seminal principles." God not only made the atoms but provided them with motion, and the law of that motion determines their subsequent fate and therefore automatically implies the realization of the final ends God set himself; the genesis of things is implicit in the atoms and their motion. Thus in Gassendi we see efficient causes and final causes assimilated into a single system; he offers a version of atomism that leaves room for the teleological view next to the deterministic one. A continual intervention of God is now no longer necessary; what he does acknowledge is that the world, which did not originate "of its own," now continues in accordance with the laws that God not only gave but also upholds. To uphold, however, is something quite other than to intervene: God has given things their laws *once for all!*

In the Cartesian system, however, only extension belongs to the essence of matter, and not motion. There, matter is dead and inert; motion comes to it from the outside; final causes therefore fit less well in the Cartesian picture. Accordingly, should one still wish to account for the origin of the complicated, more highly organized "machines" found in nature, one is forced much sooner to have recourse to immediate divine interventions. This consequence can indeed be seen in occasionalism, which requires a constant intervention on the part of God, thus turning the process of nature into one continuous miracle, a view which Boyle (as we hope to show below) repudiates.

Another solution was sought by Ralph Cudworth (1619–88) in his *True Intellectual System of the Universe*. Cudworth is a vehement opponent of the mechanical philosophy insofar as it ventures outside science; within science he considers it of great importance for the explanation of phenomena. His conception of matter leans toward Cartesianism; that is to say, the material particles do not carry within them the law that determines their future. Cudworth equally rejects chance. His problem, therefore, is that he has difficulty ascribing the origin of certain substances, of plants and animals, to a dead and inert matter. Yet he judges a constant intervention of God to be a continuous miracle and thus not conformable to God's majesty. He now resorts to a *vis plastica,* a kind of world-soul which is the principle of motion and life and which stands between God, who conceives the law of every body, and matter, which is formed according to that law. Without this plastic medium the Cartesian view, Cudworth recognizes, would lead to the assumption of a continuous miracle. However, in Boyle's critique of "nature," all such principles—which have the function of a demiurge ("semi-deities"), whether they be called world-soul, nature, or plastic power—are dismissed (without mentioning Cudworth) as utter unnecessities, which of course is what they are, on his conception, a conception for which he does not (oddly enough) refer to Gassendi, even though it has close affinity with Gassendi's.

There is still another argument that is urged against God's providence, an argument which is more concerned with the ethical realm and which points especially to the non-purposefulness of things. The teleological argument may adduce sublime reasons why everything accommodates itself so purposefully to the use and comfort of man and beast, but even in Boyle's days there were people who thought that a sheep just might not consider the teeth of a wolf all that purposeful and that earthquakes and other natural disasters do not exactly serve the utility of man.

Against these objections Boyle invokes the end of the *whole.* The interest of the individual must give way to the interest of the community; the lesser makes way for the greater.[1] But this hardly excuses earthquakes, for they profit no one! Is the world really "the best of all worlds," as Voltaire, mocking Leibniz, would refer to it later, after the earthquake of Lisbon?

As a believer Boyle replies: Yes it is, because *God* made her.[2] But that is where he stops; the teleological appetite for ratiocination does not impel him to portray everything as "intelligible" or to excuse it to the mind. It is not the *best* world in which we live just because we *perceive* it to be so, or because God could not act otherwise.[3] Against those who reject divine providence on account of the "irregularities" in nature (catastrophes, famine, monsters) Boyle forbears offering teleological counterarguments. He is not cynical enough to see in them a remedy for overpopulation. He pleads that God is a sovereign

---

[1] *The Notion of Nature*; 5:199, 251f.
[2] Ibidem; 197.
[3] Ibidem; 195–97.

Creator, perfectly free to make the world according to *his* good
pleasure and not bound by any necessity whatsoever.[1]

Why this world should be good is not entirely clear to the
understanding, because while God made some of his purposes known
at creation (such as the manifestation of his glory), others he "hid in
the abyss of the divine wisdom and counsels"[2]:

> If we set aside the consideration of miracles, as things supernatural,
> and of those instances wherein the providence of the great Rector
> of the universe and human affairs is pleased peculiarly to interpose;
> it may be rationally said that God, having an infinite understanding
> to which all things are at once in a manner present, did, by virtue
> of it, clearly discern what would happen in consequence of the laws
> by him established, in all the possible combinations of them, and
> in all the junctures of circumstances wherein the creatures con-
> cerned in them may be found. And that having . . . settled among
> his corporeal works, general and standing laws of motion suited to
> his most wise ends, it seems very congruous to his wisdom to
> prefer . . . catholic laws and uniformity in his conduct before
> making changes in it according to every sort of particular emergen-
> cies; and consequently, not to recede from the general laws He at
> first most wisely established, to . . . prevent some seeming
> irregularities (such as earthquakes, floods, famines, etc.), which
> are no other than such as He foresaw would happen . . . and
> thought fit to ordain, or to permit, as not unsuitable to some or
> other of those wise ends which He may have in his all-pervading
> view, . . . divers of which, for aught we can tell, are known only
> to himself; whence we may argue that several phaenomena which
> seem to us anomalous, may be very conducive to those secret ends,
> and therefore are unfit to be censured by us dim-sighted mortals.[3]

The world is an epistle of which "some parts are written in plain
characters, others in cyphers." Now if a man finds that the plainest
passages appear excellently suited to the particular purposes they were
designed for, then it is rational as well as equitable for him to conclude
that this is true also of the illegible passages. And so God "does both
gratify our understandings, and make us sensible of the imperfection of
them."[4]

---

[1] Here, indeed, will triumphs over law, over reason.

[2] *The Notion of Nature;* 5:198.

[3] Ibidem; 251f.

[4] Ibidem; 252.

This is a motif that Pascal too (and much more strikingly) seizes upon, with a shift of emphasis to the irrational: there is too much in nature to say that there is no God, too little to be able to see Him always and everywhere with certainty.[1]

Boyle warns against a rational teleology that is taken too far. Earthquakes that destroy so many people, fruit trees overcharged with fruit so that they die—these are not exactly the best illustrations, he says, of the optimistic proverb, "Nature always does what is best." And if one does not look at just one particular thing, say the eye, but takes the welfare of the whole universe into purview, then the argument from design can often not be made.[2]

When it comes to earthquakes, on which the "natural light" apparently cannot shed any light for Boyle either, he draws on special revelation for an answer. Scripture teaches that the whole creation groans under the consequences of the Fall, which include natural disasters.[3] When all teleology fails, Boyle finally reaches for his Bible to get an answer.

§ 3. Critique of the Philosophers

Boyle is a zealous defender of the mechanical philosophy. He is very much aware, however, which part of it belongs to scientific theory and which part lies entirely within the domain of worldview. Just as he himself in his experimental work and its scientific explication never derives preconceptions from his religious worldview, just as little does he want mechanical philosophers to mix their atheistic or deistic biases with natural science.[4] To be sure, in his own work the acceptance of the creation and the providence of God precedes his mechanical philosophy, but it stands outside the scientific theory. As a scientist he abstracts from all immaterial beings (whose existence he is quite happy to acknowledge) and from all supernatural and miraculous events (although he fully believes in them).[5] He pleads for a natural philosophy that covers only the field of purely material things[6]; he contemplates the course of nature "as a naturalist, without invading the

---

[1] Literally: "ni une présence manifeste, ni une exclusion totale." *Pensées,* nr. 556.

[2] *The Notion of Nature;* 5:226.

[3] Ibidem; 198.

[4] *The Usefulness of Natural Philosophy;* 2:58.

[5] *The Mechanical Hypothesis;* 4:71.

[6] Ibidem; 72.

province of the divines by intermeddling with supernatural mysteries,"[1] and he quotes Sir Francis Bacon's warning against "unwisely mingling and confounding theology and philosophy."[2] He desires a natural science that does not search for the *first* causes but only for the subsequent ones. He believes that God provided matter with motion and that this motion of the particles led to the world as we know it. He says: God provided the models, as it were, and instituted those rules of motion and order of things which we call natural laws. If one but acknowledges that the universe was once framed by God, was endowed by him with laws of motion, and ever since has been upheld by his *"incessant concourse and general providence,"* then one may consider the phenomena of nature to be *physically* produced by the "mechanical affections of the parts of matter, and what they operate upon one another according to mechanical laws."[3]

Only the latter fall within the domain of Boyle's physics. Accordingly, physics poses no danger in religious questions. A corpuscular philosophy, kept within the reasonable bounds of physical experience, may not only be admitted without falling into the Epicurean error but can even be employed *against* it.[4] For that matter, Boyle is firmly convinced that the more one engages in *experimental* philosophy, in science grounded in trials instead of in speculation, the more one is disposed to hear the voice of God.[5]

a. The Uncertainty of Natural Philosophy
But what do the "modern" philosophers do? Instead of applying their philosophy where it is applicable, they forge of it a weapon against religion. At that point, Boyle, who is normally a fervent defender of Epicurus and Descartes, becomes a vehement opponent of their atheistic and deistic adherents. In his opposition he recognizes with them the right of reason to act as judge in matters both of science and religion, for reason is the "most excellent possession of the human spirit." But for him the right use of reason entails the recognition of its own limitations. Consequently, when religion is attacked in the name of science because it is not rational enough, Boyle decides to examine to what degree natural philosophy itself is as rational as it demands of

---

[1] *The Origin of Forms and Qualities;* 3:7.

[2] *The Usefulness of Natural Philosophy;* 2:57f, quoting *The Advancement of Learning,* bk. I.

[3] *The Mechanical Hypothesis;* 4:68f; emphasis added.

[4] *The Possibility of the Resurrection;* 4:192.

[5] See below, chap. IV.

religion, and then, to what degree philosophical certainty can be compared to religious certainty. In this way he wants to administer a healthy blow to the rationalistic self-assurance of atheists and deists.

When the latter claim that it is inconceivable that there is a God and assert that atomistic philosophy alone makes everything clear and distinct, then one should not mark their self-assurance so much as the *principles* of natural philosophy itself. For then it will become apparent that the difficulty to conceive any of God's attributes, such as his eternity, "proceeds not so much from any absurdity belonging to the notion of a Deity as such, as from the difficulty which our dim human intellects find to conceive the nature of those first things which, to be the causes of all others, must be themselves without cause."[1] "Finite understandings are not able clearly to resolve such difficulties as exact a clear comprehension of what is really *infinite.*"[2]

Thus Boyle does not impute the deficiency in rationality to the object of knowledge but to the knowing subject. If explanation is to subsume things under more inclusive concepts, then the understanding cannot but come to a halt before the fundamental principles. For that matter, that was just as true for the atomists!

An atomist himself, Boyle continues, is compelled to allow the eternity of matter, the origin of motion, the infinity of space, and the limited divisibility of matter into atoms, atoms which he must confess to be present in infinite number, in an infinite variety of shapes, and to be moving downwards from eternity. In thus denying God the atomist is unable to free his understanding from those puzzling difficulties which he advances as the reasons for his denial: he affirms, not of one God but of an infinite number of atoms, that they are eternal, self-existent, immortal and self-moving; meanwhile he makes so many assumptions encumbered with difficulties that they engross him completely and make him accustomed to them.[3] All these things, however, were *assumed* by Epicurus, not *proved.*[4]

Accordingly, if one ascends to the first general causes—matter, motion, shape and size of particles—they cannot be accounted for satisfactorily without acknowledging an "intelligent author and disposer of things."[5] Every attempt at explaining them, says Boyle, ends either in no explanation at all, or in the acceptance of an intelligent Creator.

---

[1] *The Usefulness of Natural Philosophy;* 2:59.

[2] *The Christian Virtuoso;* 5:515.

[3] *The Usefulness of Natural Philosophy;* 2:59.

[4] Ibidem; 2:42.

[5] Ibidem; 2:37.

And since he perceives such an abundance of intelligence displayed in nature, his own choice is not doubtful.

Even where it concerns those first principles that do not lie entirely within the sphere of the infinite, it is still a matter, says Boyle, of accepting without understanding. Attempts at analyzing these concepts more closely fail to yield any certainty. On that score atomists, Cartesians and Aristotelians face the same perplexity.

Boyle points out that matter or corporeality may seem very familiar to us yet our *conception* of it "has been very hotly disputed of." Descartes says that "the nature of a body consists in extension every way," but other metaphysicians assert that impenetrability belongs to it as well. Nor has the controversy *de compositione continui* been settled: both conceptions, atomism *or* infinite divisibility of matter, lead to absurdities. Though we do not clearly understand the nature of body in general, yet "we cannot but be perfectly acquainted" with particular bodies. At the same time, "we know very little of the manner by which our senses inform us" of them. The union of body and soul is difficult to conceive; in what manner an incorporeal substance determines the motion of a corporeal substance is not clear. We do not comprehend why one thing produces a sensation of "whiteness," another of "yellowness," just as we do not comprehend "why melody and sweet things do generally delight us." There is no other answer "but that it was the good pleasure of the Author of nature to have it so."[1]

But the Aristotelians are no better, from Boyle's point of view. Instead of concepts they always come up with words. With their "substantial forms" they do no more than just note the facts once again: explanation is advanced not one whit. Nevertheless the mechanical philosophers have no reason to boast of the comparative certainty and clarity of their knowledge, for "as the Aristotelians cannot particularly show how their qualities are produced, so we cannot particularly explicate how they are perceived."[2]

Thus Boyle recognizes the puzzling nature of the "ordinary" phenomena that we are so familiar with. He shows, perhaps somewhat gloatingly, that the philosophy of these "simple" things has its sects too, among which not even reason can decide. The enigmatic nature of the human personality and of the power of beauty to move us has not escaped him, and despite his great confidence in the mechanical philosophy he does not arrogantly venture to give an explication of

---

[1] *The Excellency of Theology;* 4:43f.
[2] Ibidem; 45.

them in terms of atoms. Boyle the *experimental* philosopher, in contrast to the speculative metaphysicians, has learned to accept facts even when he does not understand them!

Even when science does not overstep its bounds but restricts itself to explanation in terms of "secondary" causes, it still has every reason to remain modest, according to Boyle. We are far from understanding each and every secondary (i.e., not metaphysical, but purely physical) cause. The propagation of animals is a mystery for the atomist too; mercury defies all attempts at chemical analysis. And if we go from the Epicureans to the "modern" peripatetics, who likewise accept a world without God, then we encounter mere *words:* "Gold sinks in quicksilver through gravity." Something as universal as gravity, they think, everybody will be able to understand. Well, the effect of gravity is obvious enough, but the cause of gravity, its "nature," has given us so much difficulty that no one has been able to explain it.[1]

Another argument that Boyle uses to urge science not to be "puffed up" is based on its incompleteness. Everything in nature is woven into a single whole, he argues; therefore, to have perfectly certain knowledge one would really have to know the *whole.* At present, however, many influences on experiments and observations remain unknown. Moreover, similar phenomena can have different causes. One is never finished reading the Book of Nature; no physicist is conscious of having understood the *whole.*

And then, he continues, Reason just tries to fill in what is lacking in experience. The clever, rational system of Aristotle still seemed correct one day, only to be toppled the next by an historical (hence contingent, non-rational) discovery: Jupiter was observed to have satellites![2] The torrid zone was held to be uninhabitable, and that not on flimsy grounds: yet modern navigation showed how erroneous this view was.[3] In short, Boyle sees that Reason fails and simple experience walks away with the honors: great discoveries like gunpowder, glass, the magnetic compass, were not produced by philosophy but were lighted on by chance. A comprehensive world system like that of the Cartesians can therefore only continue its flights of fancy with impunity until it is checked by experience: what the Cartesians teach about the interior of the earth or about interstellar space is uncertain and almost as difficult to prove false as true, since these opinions do

---

[1] *The Usefulness of Natural Philosophy;* 2:36f.

[2] *The Excellency of Theology;* 4:49, 60.

[3] Ibidem; 48, 59.

not admit of experimental proof but only of accommodation to one's particular hypothesis.[1]

We could say the same today about a number of biological and geological theories!

b. The Certainty of Science and Theology
Having thus brought physical certainty back within its confines, Boyle next examines the question whether theology affords less certainty. The common view of his day is: physics has greater certainty; in theological matters different opinions are possible, else there would not be so many sects.

This last comment does not embarrass Boyle. As we have seen, he shows how natural philosophy too has its sects, which disagree on the very fundamentals.

We might expect him to appeal in addition to the difference in character between scientific and religious certainty, but we have shown already how he summons every issue, in science and religion alike, before the bar of Reason. So he is not going to take the modern way out. No, he is going to demonstrate: (1) that what is considered uncertain in religion belongs to the non-essentials; (2) that the uncertainty of religion is of the same kind as that of science.

On the first point the "latitudinarian" in Boyle offers the following commentary. Granted, there are many sects, but the fundamental and necessary articles of religion are evident and capable of demonstration: no right-thinking Christians will disagree on them. Confidently he continues:

> And if there be any articles of religion for which a rational or cogent proof cannot be brought, *I shall for that very reason conclude, that such articles are not absolutely necessary to be believed;* since it seems no way reasonable to imagine that God, having been pleased to send not only his prophets and his apostles but his only son into the world, to promulgate to mankind the Christian religion . . . and to alter the course of nature by numerous miracles, that it might be believed; it seems not unreasonable, I say, to imagine that he should not propose those truths . . . with at least so much clearness, as that studious and well-disposed readers may certainly understand such as are necessary for them to believe.[2]

---

[1] *The Excellency of Theology*; 4:50–52.
[2] Ibidem; 41 (emphasis added).

What a distance separates us here from Pascal! Where is the God who dwells in secret and who reveals himself only to his elect? What blurring of the boundaries between common and special grace! Is faith then for Boyle, at least insofar as it is necessary, rational? It would almost seem that his position resembles the deism he so detests!

But we must not think either that faith for Boyle is a mathematical problem; nothing of what he says necessarily means that faith is capable of "metaphysical," absolute proof. To judge him correctly we must listen to his exposition of the second point and take a closer look at what he understands by "certainty."

Boyle makes use of the distinction, also common among the scholastics, between metaphysical, physical and historical certainty. Metaphysical certainty is absolute: it is impossible that the thing believed should be other than true; for instance, an accomplished fact cannot be undone. Physical proofs, however, require only physical certainty, that is to say, "a certainty upon supposition that the principles of physics be true." The physical proofs of the ancients about the causes of material events rested upon the premise that "nothing is made out of nothing." Physically speaking this may be readily admitted, because in the course of nature as we observe it, nothing is ever made out of nothing; yet in a general sense it may be false (as everyone who accepts the creation of the world recognizes). So, "there being no contradiction implied in the nature of the thing" that would exclude the contrary of that premise, every unprejudiced reasoner must also allow the possibility of creation, or the possibility of bodily resurrection. Now Boyle points out that much passes for physical certainty that has no right to that claim: "most even of the modern virtuosi are wont to fancy more of clearness and certainty in their physical theories than a critical examiner will find."[1] It is in this context that he discusses the uncertainty about the nature of sensation and corporeal substance, and the famous controversy *de compositione continui*.

He remarks that there are "I know not how many things in physics, that men presume they believe upon physical and cogent arguments, wherein they really have but a moral assurance." Since he says also about *historical* proofs (for example, of the truth of religion) that they have a "moral certainty," for all practical purposes his view comes down to this, that physics is for the greater part "historical"—a standpoint that follows from his view of a "natural history" that is to form the basis of natural philosophy. As a rule, Boyle argues, we accept the correctness of a scientific observation and an historical fact

[1] Ibidem; 42.

alike on the testimony of others, and consequently their certainty is of the same kind:

> . . . in many things that are looked upon as physical demonstrations there is really but a moral certainty. For when, for instance, Descartes and other modern philosophers take upon them to demonstrate that there are divers comets that are not meteors because they have a parallax lesser than that of the moon, and are of such a bigness, and some of them move in such a line, etc., it is plain that [these natural philosophers] had never the opportunity to observe a comet in their lives . . . And though the inferences as such may have a demonstrable certainty, yet the premises they are drawn from having but an historical one, the presumed physico-mathematical demonstration can produce in a wary mind but a moral certainty . . . [1]

Physical experiments, moreover, are so difficult to perform, according to Boyle, and so difficult to reproduce accurately, that theories based on experiments can hardly have more than a "moral" certainty; they lack the "exactness that is requisite for the building of an undoubted theory upon them."[2]

As noted earlier, Boyle demonstrates that in physics the discovery of facts precedes their deduction by reason (gunpowder, Jupiter's satellites).[3] Accordingly he does not consider it a valid objection that in theology, too, not everything can be independently discovered by reason, by the "light of nature," but that it rests in part on historical revelation. In his view, then, this would be comparable to the discoveries "by chance." Yet those discoveries and that historical, special revelation may well, in Boyle's train of thought, be apprehended rationally afterward! For Boyle, then, just as science rests on a "natural history" so religion rests on "redemptive history." Both rest on a testimony of what has been seen or heard.[4]

First of all, therefore, the "historical" nature of religion has its parallel in science. But, secondly, there is a parallel in the nature of their respective fundamental principles. Physics comprehends, say, "matter" the least, although it is very certain about its existence. In the same way God's existence is perfectly certain for Boyle, but he is

---

[1] *The Excellency of Theology*; 4:42.

[2] Ibidem.

[3] Ibidem; 49.

[4] Ibidem; 48f.

equally certain of God's incomprehensibility.[1] Accordingly he denies science the right to reproach religion for the incomprehensibility of its highest Object.

In the third place, Boyle is unwilling, in science, to entertain the question, Why *this* world and not another? Similarly, in theology he is unwilling to take up the question, Why does God follow *this* way of redemption and not another? In both cases it is enough for him, evidently, that God willed it so. God does not hold to this order because it is good, but it is good because God held to it![2]

It is these points of similarity that prompt Boyle to declare that the imperfection of our knowledge about physical matters ought to be enough "to keep us from being puffed up . . . and from undervaluing upon its account the study of the mysteries of divinity . . . "[3]

Thus he has shown that physics has only a "moral certainty" rather than being rational through and through. In the same way, he says, only a "moral certainty" may be demanded of theology, which is "enough for a wise man, and even a philosopher [after what has been said about physical things] to acquiesce in."[4]

In physics and religion, therefore, Boyle appeals in true Baconian fashion to the empirical and contingent nature of much of human knowledge. He submits that our knowledge is not very deep and does not reach with any certainty "to the bottom of things," nor does it penetrate to their innermost nature. Neither does it know *why* things are the way they are and not otherwise; why there are so many stars in some parts of the sky and so few in others; why those celestial lights are not placed in more orderly patterns but seem to be scattered in the sky as it were by chance.[5] Boyle recognizes that we arrive at no true *episteme*; that we are simply to start with what is given and extract from it rules and laws without learning of their why or wherefore; that we must be content with *pistis*, a form of knowledge based on "moral

---

[1] See *Seraphic Love;* 1:264 and *The Usefulness of Natural Philosophy;* 2:59.

[2] This is how we think we may interpret Boyle's view. It is a point on which his contemporaries are not agreed; the Cambridge Platonists asserted that good and evil, right and wrong are *physei*, not *thesei*, thus that there is no Divine arbitrariness. Lechler, *Geschichte des englischen Deismus*, p. 133.

[3] *The Excellency of Theology;* 4:45.

[4] Ibidem; 42.

[5] Ibidem; 50f.

certainty."[1] That is also why he can accept the imperfection of our knowledge of God; here too we walk in faith, not yet in understanding. Nevertheless he does say that, since its object is so much nobler, a "dim knowledge of God" is to be preferred to a "clearer knowledge of those inferior truths that physics is wont to teach."[2]

---

[1] Cf. Plato's *Republic,* 511e, with its four ascending gradations of knowledge: from *doxa* (opinion), consisting of *eikasia* (imagination) and *pistis* (faith), to *episteme* (knowledge), subdivided over *dianoia* (comprehension) and *noesis* (reason).

[2] *The Excellency of Theology;* 4:47.

Chapter IV

SPECIAL REVELATION

§ 1. The Necessity of a Special Revelation

The expression "natural religion" often sounds so unpleasant in our ears because we associate it with a purely intellectual faith, constructed by human reason which not only can err but for which it is presumptuous pride to make statements on its own about a God who, if he exists, must infinitely transcend all human thought. But we have seen that in Boyle natural religion is ultimately revealed religion; it does not spring from any "metaphysical" considerations of the human intellect but is bound to the empirically given *revelation in nature* which is not rationally perspicuous. It cannot be said of Boyle: "If he had made the world he would have done so exactly like God." In his natural religion, too, he comes to confess that "My thoughts are not your thoughts." Nevertheless, man is "God's offspring" and consequently Boyle believes that up to a point Reason is able to judge, provided it submits to Experience and recognizes its own limits. The latter condition places Boyle in opposition to the non-orthodox adherents of a natural religion, the deists, who overestimate Reason. Nor does he, like the deists, halt at natural religion; rather, on "rational" grounds he is bound to acknowledge the possibility of a "special" revelation.

Natural religion brought man to the acknowledgment that God is his Creator and Provider and that therefore he owes him veneration and obedience. In consequence Boyle finds it reasonable that God has given man a law in conformity with which he can as a rational creature perform those duties that are most pleasing to God. Thus the acknowledgment of Providence, who also speaks in sacred history, is for Boyle the "bridge whereon one may pass from natural to revealed religion"[1]: natural theology, he writes, affords us great knowledge of God and reveals many of his attributes, but what God has revealed to us about himself in a direct way is far preferable to what we can discover ourselves by the dim light of nature. Revelation is therefore for us a telescope for our weak eyes and that is why illiterate men like the first Christians could have more suitable conceptions about God than the greatest philosophers who had to do without that revelation. Hence much more is revealed to us about God by the Book of Scripture than by the Book of Nature. For Scripture gives us historical accounts of God's thoughts and actions; the saints of the Old Testament are mentioned to us by God in their frailties and sin in order to encourage us and to teach us that not only prophets, saints and martyrs but also "multitudes of more imperfect servants" have access to him. The light of Reason may teach us something about God's nature; special Revelation deepens that knowledge and discloses his will, or positive laws.[2]

But there is more. Many things there are which "bare reason," owing to its weakness, is unable, even in part, to discover on its own; yet once they are presented through special revelation reason can readily embrace them.[3] To these belong God's sovereign decrees and the future state of mankind.[4] Reason teaches us much about the human soul; but it does not regard immortality as necessary. The ordering hand of God at the birth of the cosmos is recognized by many philosophers (final causes), but the creation of matter (as chaos) is accepted only on the basis of a revelation. Nor can unassisted reason inform us of particulars about the origin of the world; here Scripture affords valuable hints.[5] We do not know the mysteries of the Trinity or of redemption apart from Revelation.[6]

With this last we have arrived at matters that *transcend* reason, also on Boyle's view. What we discussed just now were things that reason does not discover on its own, although they fall within its reach afterward, just as in science many discoveries are made by accident rather than on grounds of rational deduction.

---

[1] *The Christian Virtuoso;* 5:522.

[2] *The Excellency of Theology;* 4:7-9.

[3] *Things Above Reason;* 4:406f. *The Excellency of Theology;* 4:9.

[4] *Things Above Reason;* 4:406.

[5] *The Excellency of Theology;* 4:11. *The Usefulness of Natural Philosophy;* 2:19.

[6] *The Excellency of Theology;* 4:15.

§ 2. The Supernatural

a. The "Rational" View of Miracles

If revealed religion deals with that which cannot be discovered by the natural light of reason, this does not diminish the fact that reason perceives afterward that revealed religion is rational, insofar as rationality is possible. Boyle's meaning is best illustrated in his consideration of miracles, in particular the miracle of the bodily resurrection.[1] There he begins by saying that he would never have thought of such a thing as a "resurrection" if God had not positively revealed it in Scripture: it cannot occur but by the power of God, and it cannot be known or demonstrated by the mere light of nature; so that cannot be the issue. Nor is the issue whether this miracle can be brought to pass by merely "physical" agents, for the experience of the ages teaches that it is not in accordance with the common course of nature. Boyle wishes merely to demonstrate that "in speculation" it is not *absolutely* repugnant to reason that the scattered parts of a dead body come together again; "morally," to ordinary human reason, it is impossible.[2]

If resurrection from the dead were absolutely impossible, it would be irrational on Boyle's view, and that he does not want. He removes the "offense" from the miracle, yet that does not mean it ceases to be a miracle! For he acknowledges that a resurrection requires an immediate act of God effected by his own power[3]: God's omnipotence extends to all that is not truly contradictory to the nature of God himself or to the things he created.[4]

When Epicurus asserts, says Boyle, that a body once dead cannot be made alive again by reason of the dissipation and dispersion of the atoms it was composed of when alive, then this assertion is *physically* demonstrable. Yet the contrary may be true if God's omnipotence intervenes, as when Lazarus was raised from the dead: "all unprejudiced reasoners must allow it to be possible, there being no contradiction implied in the nature of the thing."[5]

---

[1] *The Excellency of Theology;* 4:12, 42. *The Possibility of the Resurrection;* 4:192.

[2] *The Possibility of the Resurrection;* 4:192.

[3] Ibidem.

[4] Ibidem; 201.

[5] *The Excellency of Theology;* 4:42.

Boyle means that the resurrection of a dead body is not absolutely impossible in the atomistic line of thought, but only exceedingly improbable. We would be mistaken, however, if we looked in him for the modern statistical views, which claim to have expelled causal reasoning. He is not trying to explain away the miracle by saying that according to the theory of probability once in an odd while, say, an object will not fall; he does not belong to those respectable orthodox folk who hate to appear to be "behind the times" and who greedily snatch at scientific explanations of the miracle of the Red Sea or the unfortunate accident of Lot's wife; his attempts do not end in "wonders no miracles."[1]

No, Boyle would sooner regard all nature as a "miracle," for it is one concatenation of improbabilities. When Epicurus has the animal species and the whole cosmos arise by Chance, then Boyle appeals to the extremely high improbability of such a chance occurrence, and infers from that the immediate intervention of God in the composition of the world. But improbabilities of this kind he wants to keep outside *physical science:* neither the creation events nor miracles fall within the physical order for him. Nevertheless, even the physical order has something that is not absolutely rational *for us*. It is possible, therefore, that God infringes upon that order without doing anything that is anti-rational in an absolute sense. All of Boyle's reasoning displays this latitude. As God possesses absolute Reason and we partake of it only imperfectly, we can sometimes see the rationality of God's work, but at other times we cannot. In the latter case, however, Boyle does not think that this makes it irrational!

Now God, to be sure, has instituted the rules, the "laws of nature," according to which created miracles occur (else Boyle would have to consider the study of nature impossible). Yet God is also able to interfere again in that clockwork and bring about what is highly improbable according to the sovereignly imposed laws currently in force.

At the ordering of the atoms into the cosmos God according to his good pleasure gave the laws that we see operative in mechanical causality; by the same token, in a miracle he breaks through that mechanical causality. In so doing he does nothing contradictory to reason; it does not militate against nature that the same atoms once more compose the same body; but that those atoms would do so if left to themselves is *physically* impossible; when that occurs a *miracle* takes

---

[1] [Cf. *Life;* 1:lxxxv.]

place! This is approximately how we may picture Boyle's train of thought.

Boyle does his best to show in what way the miracle of the resurrection might be produced.[1] In all these efforts at absolving religion before the bar of science some doubt may be operative. Particularly in the 19th century, when scientific materialism reigned supreme, the orthodox came up with some rather materialistic explanations of miracles which today strike one as a concession to unbelief.

Boyle's arguments, too, contain much that is weak. Nor does he improve his case when in another place he compares God's intervention in nature to the human mind which—not subject to mechanical causality—governs the body. For now we run into the thorny problem of predestination and free will. Granted that God sometimes suspends mechanical causality, does the human mind, too, overrule causality in the body and, through its actions, that of all nature? Here Boyle confuses two terrains, although he usually sees clearly that this is illegitimate and that these two terrains must be viewed alongside each other, not through each other. The Cartesians struggled with the same problem, and the occasionalists actually ended up saying that every event is a miracle, a direct intervention of God.

Boyle wants to demonstrate the possibility of the bodily resurrection, namely that it is not contrary to what reason regards as the "nature" of bodies. But even here he cannot remain consistent: he says of "glorified" bodies that they have "preternatural qualities." In them God has suspended the natural action of bodies; the Author of the laws of nature may change them in his omnipotence (the iron axe-head floated on the water; Peter walked on the waves).[2] Once again Boyle sees no contradiction: lightness and transparency are but "mechanical affections" of matter.[3] But if this is no contradiction, we wonder what is? What then is a body separated from its "affections"?

b. The Historical View of Miracles

Far more attractive than these rational "proofs" of miracles seem to us his empirical, historical proofs. Here Boyle invokes the *realism* that ought to characterize the physicist as well as the Christian. The truth of the Christian religion, according to him, is founded upon the excellency of its doctrine, upon historical facts—"the divine miracles

---

[1] *The Mechanical Hypothesis;* 4:73.

[2] *The Possibility of the Resurrection;* 4:201.

[3] Ibidem.

that were wrought to recommend it"—and upon the effects it produced
in the world.[1] For the latter, too, point to supernatural aid: the religion
of "but half a score of illiterate fishermen and a few tent-makers and
other tradesmen" was spread over a great part of the then known world
without force of arms or any allurements save the prediction of
hardships and persecutions. This "wonderful quick progress" is an
argument afforded by experience,[2] just as miracles are.

Experience, Boyle continues, is gained not only personally but
also historically, through what others communicate. We know a
"revelation" only through a *testimony,* not through a *ratiocination.* Now
in science we scruple not to believe many things through experience
(gained either immediately or vicariously, upon the testimony of others)
which apart from that experience would be judged unfit to be believed
or even contrary to reason. It was judged contrary to reason that a body
ten times the weight should not fall ten times as fast.[3] For centuries it
was judged repugnant to reason that there should be generations or
corruptions in the heavens; yet today sun spots have been discovered
and although not everyone has seen them everyone accepts them "upon
the credit of those that have observed them."[4] In the same way we
ought to bow to everything that rests on real experience, even if it be
supernatural. If in physical questions we have to accept many things on
the strength of other people's testimony or personal observation which
earlier seemed non-rational or even irrational, then we ought certainly
to do so in supernatural questions.[5] And the apostles were eye-
witnesses of the miracles of Christ. Do we scientists not consult
seafarers about America, even though they be illiterate? An ordinary
seaman who sailed with Columbus was able to rectify the erroneous
assumptions of the peripatetic philosophers.[6]

To bow to the facts, Boyle argues, even if they *seem* irrational,
is surely the first requirement of reason. The proofs that natural
theology affords of God's existence and attributes, he notes, are highly
to be prized; but whether they be derived from a metaphysical concept
like innate ideas or from a philosophical contemplation of nature,[7] they
are to him inferior to those that are grounded on immediate experience

---

[1] *The Christian Virtuoso;* 5:524.

[2] Ibidem; 533.

[3] Ibidem; 526f.

[4] Ibidem; 528.

[5] Ibidem; 529.

[6] Ibidem; 530.

[7] Ibidem.

or "historical" facts. Thus once again Boyle's realism prevails over his rationalism.

Miracles and fulfilled prophecies, says Boyle, are to a rational human being the best proofs of God's existence and providence and of the truth of the Christian religion. In particular the miracles wrought by Christ, notably his rising from the dead, are sufficient to overthrow atheism. There are so many testimonies to the truth of these facts that they cannot be denied without denying reason itself.[1]

Whoever acknowledges this revelation will also be happy to accept the more hidden, abstruse articles of the Christian religion.[2] Among these Boyle includes the Trinity, the Incarnation, the work of the Holy Spirit, and Predestination.[3] However, the emphasis in Boyle lies entirely on the "historical" facts. To his mind, the dogmas of the Trinity and Predestination must have been "to a far lesser extent" the data of religious experience (personal or through historical testimony). They are too speculative: he also deems it destructive to enter upon them too deeply; that only creates division and uncertainty.

Nowhere in Boyle do we find these dogmas defended at length, which we do in the case of the "historical" miracles. Boyle exhibits the same reluctance here as he showed in physics to decide in questions where reason sees more than one possibility while experience has nothing to contribute (e.g., the nature of a vacuum). An obscure *event,* however, be it in natural history or in salvation history, we have but to accept in its unmistakable reality and then, if possible, to interpret rationally afterward.

In any case, it is typical of Western Christianity that it puts so much emphasis on the historicity of the redemptive facts. In this, Boyle remains in line with the Church which (like him) has particularly made the acknowledgment of the reality of Christ's resurrection a shibboleth of orthodoxy.

c. Rational Empiricism

Boyle champions a kind of rational empiricism. Not a shallow empiricism that collects facts without sifting them; this he repudiates in theology as much as in science. But still, we must always start with the facts. We cannot deduce a natural philosophy out of ourselves: if there are any innate ideas, they are so few in number that we cannot come to know the complex system of the world through ratiocination, without

---

[1] *The Usefulness of Natural Philosophy;* 2:58f.

[2] Ibidem; 59.

[3] *The Style of Holy Scripture;* 2:267.

experience.[1] Even less can we deduce religion out of ourselves, for its object is so much more exalted: abstract reasoning about God "must not only be almost always very deficient, but will be oftentimes very erroneous."[2]

At once Boyle anticipates the objection that he ascribes so much to experience that reason is degraded and made "servilely to obey."[3] Be that as it may, the school of experimental philosophy has taught him that a good reasoner will renounce the most cogent ratiocination for a single experience that contradicts it.[4]

Abstract reason "reaches but to a very small share of the multitude of things knowable," Boyle maintains, and he considers this to be the case in science and religion alike, for he goes on to say that reason needs the assistance of experience and supernatural revelation.[5] On the other hand, reason remains the judge of supernatural revelation, and the understanding retains the right to examine whether a testimony is indeed divine![6] Thus not only natural philosophy, and natural religion, but even revealed religion is to a certain extent "rational." That this in no way means that the Divine now fits within the framework of Reason, we shall see below.

In Boyle reason is not dethroned, but "she is obliged to take in all the assistance she can from experience, whether natural or supernatural." By the fuller information thus received, reason may "rectify, if need be, her former and less mature judgments." This is imperative, for reason is not self-sufficient.[7]

Thus the champion of a *rational-empirical science* is at the same time the man who contends for the recognition of Christianity as a *rational-empirical religion!*

d. Reason on the Suprarational

Many theologians today shudder as much at the expression "rational religion" as they do at the expression "natural theology." But we have already seen that Boyle's rational religion is both an empirical and a revealed religion. Now it might still look as though Boyle on the one hand acknowledges reason's inability to arrive at a rational religion

---

[1] *The Christian Virtuoso;* 5:538.

[2] Ibidem; 539.

[3] Ibidem; 538.

[4] Ibidem.

[5] Ibidem; 539.

[6] Ibidem; 539f.

[7] Ibidem; 540.

without empirical data (including historical data from revelation), yet on the other hand that he maintains, Scripture and Nature once given, that anyone endowed with a healthy dose of intelligence may also *a posteriori* "comprehend" everything about religious matters. The extent to which this is true or not may be learned from a review of what Boyle says about the "things that are above reason."[1]

There are things that transcend reason. Reason itself admits this, on the basis of experience first of all; secondly, on the basis of authentic testimony; and in the third place, on the basis of mathematical demonstration.[2]

Boyle calls them "priviledged things," and he divides them into three kinds.[3]

1. *Inexplicable* things. We speak of these when we cannot deny *that* they are, yet we cannot clearly and satisfactorily conceive *how* they can be such as we acknowledge they are—in other words, when the properties of a thing do not resemble any in our experience, or cannot be deduced from any agent we are acquainted with. Examples: how matter can be infinitely divisible; how spirit can move matter.

2. *Unsociable* things. With these it seems as though we have to accept contradictory statements. For example, the legal system is founded on the supposition that man has a free will and can choose not to commit criminal acts; and yet the generality of mankind ascribe to God an infallible foreknowledge of human actions.

3. *Incomprehensible* things. These are the "supra-intellectual" things whose nature is not distinctly or adequately comprehensible by us. The most important of these is the concept of God. We are probably born with—in any case have many occasions to frame—an idea of a being infinitely perfect. But upon further reflection we cannot give any greater precision to what is contained in the notion of omnipotence, omniscience, eternity, and "those other divine attributes that are all united in that great confluence and abyss of perfections, God." Short of subtle disquisitions, the mind sees at once that it is incapable of comprehending God.[4] It is presumption to imagine that we can form an adequate notion of God. We may indeed know, by the consideration of his works, including ourselves, *that he is;* we may know in a great measure *what he is not;* but to understand thoroughly

---

[1] *A Discourse of Things Above Reason* (1681); 4:406–47.

[2] *Things Above Reason;* 4:407.

[3] Ibidem; 407, 423.

[4] Ibidem; 424.

what he is surpasses our finite intellect. Thus the notion of God is
"supra-intellectual."[1]

So if we have had occasion at times to shake our heads in wonder
as Boyle indulged in lyrical celebration of the rational knowledge of
God, we are reassured when we see him enter the lists against those
people, even theologians, who, "little considering what God is, and
what [they] themselves are," presume to talk of God and his attributes
"as freely and as unpremeditately as if they were talking of a geometri-
cal figure or a mechanical engine."[2] Philosophy knows God only very
imperfectly, Boyle reminds them; it knows him only by his works,
those works are discovered only in part, and what has been discovered
is known only in part.[3] Thus little remains of the confidence with
which they claim to know God *fully* by the light of their natural
reason.[4]

But this is not to say that everything has now become clear for
Boyle in the light of special Revelation: God's wisdom and power in
the work of salvation remain incomprehensible on most counts.[5] For
that matter, God's wisdom and power in creation and providence,
which the human intellect discovers through God's works, are always
but the divine attributes as comprehended and described by the *human*
mind.[6]

In Boyle's eyes, it is a mark of ignorance as well as presumption
for us mortals "to talk of God's nature and the extent of his knowledge
as of things that we are able to look through and to measure."
Whenever we speak of God and his attributes "we ought to stand in
great awe,"[7] hence not speak irreverently of his divine essence without
considering the "immense distance betwixt God and us"[8] nor without
a deep and real sense of the "immeasurable inferiority of our best ideas
to the unbounded perfections of our Maker."[9]

Though we must not therefore have the presumption that we can
know God *fully,* nevertheless we may and must grow in the knowledge

---

[1] *Things Above Reason*; 4:408.

[2] *The Veneration Owed to God*; 5:130.

[3] Ibidem; 151.

[4] Ibidem.

[5] Ibidem; 144.

[6] Ibidem; 145.

[7] Ibidem; 156f. On Descartes' *a priori* proofs from God's Being, see ibidem;
140.

[8] *The Veneration Owed to God*; 5:157.

[9] Ibidem; 156.

of God. We must not presume to pry into God's secret counsel or his essence, yet it ought to be our humble desire to further our knowledge of him and thus heighten our reverence and devotion towards him.[1] Here Boyle thinks of Moses: though part of his request to see God was refused, "a nearer and more particular view of God . . . was vouchsafed to his holy curiosity."[2]

Boyle feels that we are so conversant with many things that we think we know them while in reality, upon closer inspection, they appear "impenetrable to reason." This is true of space, time, and motion. When we say that anything is repugnant to reason we usually mean that it is not "deducible from or consistent with one or other of those standard notions or rules" that we humans have adopted. But these rules are derived from mere finite things and may therefore be applied only to them. Hence they are deceptive and useless if we stretch them beyond their measure and apply them to the infinite God, or in general to things that are infinite in multitude, magnitude, or minuteness. Our instruments of knowledge, sensation and conception, are disproportionate to such objects.[3] Our capacity to understand is therefore not as unlimited as many philosophers suppose. Whatever self-love may say, we are but created and finite beings, we come into the world "but such as it pleased the almighty and most free author of our nature to make us," and we are furnished with but such means as God saw fit to allow us.[4] God assigned to the minds of men a bounded capacity to grasp things. Thus we may have as much knowledge as God d"thought fit to allow our minds in their present (and perchance lapsed) condition . . . "[5] Now, whether the limitation of our capacity to know is due solely to the imperfection of our earthly nature, or whether this is also influenced somehow by the Fall, is a question that Boyle prefers to leave undecided, though apparently he does not consider the latter, "perchance," impossible.

The next objection Boyle anticipates is: How can reason reach things of which it says itself that they are above reason; is that not tantamount to seeing things that are invisible?

To this he responds: Although we may not have a clear notion of some things, we may "come to be certain that they are, and so have general and dark ideas of them." When natural theology teaches us to

---

[1] Ibidem; 152.

[2] Ibidem; 152; cf. Exod. 33:18; 34:5, 6.

[3] *Things Above Reason;* 4:413f.

[4] Ibidem; 410.

[5] Ibidem; 445. According to Boyle, however, even in heaven we shall know God only very imperfectly. *Occasional Reflections;* 2:404.

believe God to be an infinitely perfect Being, we ought not to say that
we have no idea of such a being because we have not a clear and
adequate one.[1] "It is scarce possible for us to be destitute of" some
idea of God as a being, perfect and yet incomprehensible. Though we
do not speak of these things with the same confidence as we do of
things within the compass of our intellect, this need not hinder us from
speaking "rationally" of them, even though our notion of them is of
another order and quite inadequate.[2] Thus we can speak logically in
mathematics about "surd numbers" and "incommensurable magnitudes"
without knowing them clearly. We have some notion or other of God,
"that abyss of perfections,"[3] and of atoms, albeit inadequate ones.[4]
The infinite cannot be mastered; yet it may be discussed rationally; it
is not something of which we have no conception whatsoever, though
upon closer examination it confounds the intellect. I know the infinite
insofar as I know what it is *not:* not finite. Thus that which is in a
certain sense above reason, in another sense falls under it. Philosophers
are incapable of framing the true conception of bodies (of corporeal
substance in general), and yet natural philosophy does speak of bodies
and knows a great deal about them.[5]

So argues Boyle. But now this is the remarkable thing: he says,
it is by *reason* that we perceive these things to be above reason! Things
above reason must somehow make some "dark and peculiar kind of
impression" upon the understanding; for the rational soul judges of that
which lies within the compass of its faculties, but it also judges of that
which lies outside its compass. It can judge "of its own nature and
power, and discern some at least of the limits beyond which it cannot
safely exercise its act of . . . judging and defining." Our mind can
diagnose its own limits, discern its own want of light. Things above
reason are therefore not things "as our rational faculty cannot at all
reach to . . . "[6]

Accordingly, we have every right to speak of things that we know
only inadequately or through negative characteristics. The mind is so
constituted "that its faculty of drawing consequences from *known* truths

[1] *Things Above Reason;* 4:416f.
[2] Ibidem; 424, 446.
[3] Ibidem; 424.
[4] Ibidem; 445.
[5] Ibidem; 446.
[6] Ibidem; 417, 418, 422.

is of greater extent than its power of framing clear and distinct ideas of things."[1]

With this last statement Boyle has indicated the difference between a science of nature which indeed desires and does the former, and a so-called "natural philosophy" which would penetrate to the bottom of Being. The ideal of modern science can be expressed somewhat accurately, perhaps, by saying that its aim is: to determine the laws and explain the phenomena by reducing them to rules that hold for the interaction between entities that it acknowledges yet does not understand; it is satisfied with *dianoia* and forgoes *episteme*.[2] Yet the former too is valid knowledge. Boyle ends, accordingly, by concluding that we can draw up correct conclusions about things that we do not know thoroughly!

But now he hears another objection: May not these difficulties, which as yet prove insurmountable for metaphysics and mathematics (like God, soul, matter), be clarified hereafter?[3]

Boyle's answer to this is: Many things are still mysterious to us "for want of a competent history of nature" (knowledge of facts) or "by reason of erroneous prepossessions." These obstacles may be surmounted. But the metaphysical difficulties that touch neither matters of fact nor special hypotheses arise from the limited nature of our intellect. Besides, Boyle adds, future discoveries may well lead to new difficulties, "more capable than the first of baffling human understandings."[4]

The development of modern physics has proved him right. We still do not know what matter is, and—although it looks as if we have found the answer when we say, for example, that matter is electricity—how can we understand what that is in turn? We have merely exchanged the familiar supra-intellectual concept of matter for a "concept" which in its abstractness shows even better that the old difficulty, with more advanced knowledge, has been replaced by a still greater one, if that be possible.

That remarkable Eros, the lust for knowledge that desires to "contemplate" the object, as it were, in a mystical sense, that desires almost to identify itself with it, has not been satisfied. Thus Boyle is right when he remarks that the study of "priviledged things" teaches us better to know ourselves and the imperfection of our capacity to know. "I do

---

[1] Ibidem; 422; emphasis added.

[2] In Plato's *Republic*, 511e, *dianoia*, mathematical knowledge, lies midway between true, full knowledge (the actual *episteme*) and opinion (*doxa*).

[3] *Things Above Reason;* 4:412.

[4] Ibidem.

not think that it is to degrade the understanding, to refuse to idolize it;
and it is not an injury to reason to think it a limited faculty, but an
injury to the author of it to think man's understanding infinite like
his."[1]

Thus he ends with a religious self-limitation: to imagine that
through reason one is in principle on a par with the divine reason is an
arrogant presumption of the creature that wants to be like his Creator.
This motive distinguishes true religion from theosophy.

But it is also a scientific self-limitation, for as little as he
understands God, so little does he understand matter. He looks at it
with the same wonderment. This is what distinguishes true *science* from
theosophy.

As to the limits of knowledge as well, there is a parallel in Boyle
between empirical science and theology. Experience meets with
fundamentals that surpass the understanding; theology (both natural and
revealed) encounters fundamentals that surpass the understanding. In
both cases it is reason that establishes that those fundamentals surpass
reason.

Even the intellect that has been given the wings of Nature and
Scripture for its aid will see those wings melt if it thinks it can use
them to fly straight into the face of God! Theology and science both
end in Boyle with the exclamation of the psalmist: "Such knowledge is
too wonderful for me; it is high, I cannot attain unto it."[2]

§ 3. Scripture and the Confessions

a. Scripture

Let us now look more closely at the means of God's special revelation,
the Bible. According to Boyle, Scripture is indispensable for arriving
at true faith. He himself did not consider any trouble too great to
understand the Bible well. As a first precondition he posits scholarly
study, "critical learning." Really one ought to know the original
tongues, Greek and Hebrew.[3] He himself met this requirement by
learning these languages very early, in 1652, when he began his *Essay
on the Scripture.*

Further, he considers it necessary that one know the customs and
beliefs of the times and nations that the Bible speaks of. In Boyle's
opinion, it is very useful for a good understanding of the intention of

---

[1] *Things Above Reason*; 4:411.
[2] Cf. *The Veneration Owed to God;* 5:157, quoting Ps. 139:6.
[3] *The Excellency of Theology;* 4:16.

the Bible writers to be acquainted with the Talmud and the rabbinical commentaries and traditions.[1] As a result, he accepts some remarkably enlightened exegetes. St. Jude talks to the Jews about a contest between the archangel and the devil over the body of Moses—a "somewhat apocryphal" story; but, says Boyle, everyone believed it, so the apostle made use of it.[2] To understand the Mosaic laws one has to know the rites of the Sabeans, in opposition to whose magical worship many Jewish ceremonies were instituted.[3] For this view Boyle invokes the authority of Maimonides and the 17th-century antiquary Selden.

For a correct interpretation of many passages in the New Testament, according to Boyle, we have to know the persuasions and practices of the Gnostics.[4] He is conscious that the writers in the first place addressed the people of their own time, but then in such a way that all times and nations may derive profit from it.[5]

It may seem momentarily that Boyle restricts Bible study to the scholars, yet that is not his intention: God has so varied his heavenly doctrine that every sort of people can find represented in Scripture the religion in the form "they are most disposed to receive impressions from."[6] The Bible is not exclusively for a certain kind of people who "look upon their own abilities as the measure of all discourses."[7]

Thus Boyle insists on the Protestant demand: the Bible in the hands of everybody, even the lowliest. Hence his efforts at having the Bible translated into Celtic, so that also the Scottish Highlanders and the Irish might read Scripture in their own tongue. He likewise promoted the translation of the Bible for the sake of missions among the Indians of North America and he supported financially the publication of the four Gospels and Acts of the Apostles in a Malayan translation by Thomas Hyde.[8]

Boyle proceeds from the principle that Scripture, despite its difficult passages, is the means instituted by God "as well of knowledge

---

[1] That is why he always sought contact with rabbis. When as a young man (1648) he made a journey to Holland, he visited the well-known chief rabbi of the Portuguese Jews in Amsterdam, Menasseh Ben Israel, whom he refers to several times in his earliest writings; cf. 1:279; 5:183.

[2] *The Style of Holy Scripture;* 2:274.

[3] Ibidem; 265.

[4] Ibidem.

[5] Ibidem; 261.

[6] Ibidem; 263.

[7] Ibidem.

[8] *Life;* 1:cix, cxxxix, ccviii.

as of grace"; it is "one of the conduit-pipes through which God has appointed to convey his truths as well as graces."[1] This view of the Word of God as *the* means of grace is, again, typically Protestant. That we find it in the Episcopal Church indicates the strong Calvinistic and Puritan influences it had undergone. The significance of the sacraments stays in the background.

The simplest person, says Boyle, can draw the necessary knowledge from Scripture, but so can the most learned person learn his ignorance from it.[2] On the one hand, Boyle is convinced that Scripture is plain enough to teach what is needed for salvation: many texts are made dark by expositors who read their theology or metaphysics into it, while for the simple reader they are clear,[3] but on the other hand he admits that many texts in Scripture are obscure; as in science, he expects partial clarification from further study but attributes the obscurity for another part to the difficulty of the subject-matter.[4]

Now there are many, says Boyle, who reproach Scripture with its "seemingly disjointed method"; but in this it resembles the Book of Nature. There, too, God does not "suffer himself to be fettered to human laws of method," which are devised only for our own narrow conceptions. "As the heavens are higher than the earth, so are his thoughts higher than our thoughts."[5]

Here again we see Boyle's Christian realism. It is God's work, both in nature and in Scripture. Man is to accept both, just as they are, according to God's good pleasure. A different train of thought, starting from the kinship between God and man ("We are God's offspring") would try exactly that—discern human method in nature. That had been

---

[1] *The Style of Holy Scripture*; 2:269.

[2] Ibidem; 270.

[3] Too much philosophy is therefore harmful, according to Boyle: it has "perplexed the doctrine of predestination, of the trinity, of the operation of the spirit of God upon the will of man, [so as to] give advantages against those doctrines to the opposers of them." *The Style of Holy Scripture*; 2:267. Thus Boyle sees the danger that a prolonged ratiocination (as is customary in philosophy) can finally cause theology to be faced with conclusions that mock religious reality. Think only of excessive reasoning about predestination, or of the veneration of Mary. Cornelius Jansenius, bishop of Ypres, said: "Just as it has always been the mother of heretics, so philosophy is the mother of errors whenever it is applied to define the divine mysteries." Jansenius, *Augustinus*, tome II, Lib. pr. cap. 3.

[4] E.g., the Trinity; *The Style of Holy Scripture*; 2:266.

[5] Ibidem; 270; cf. Is. 55:9.

indeed the attempt of the no less orthodox Kepler.[1] But Boyle finds no harmonies in nature! For that matter, his soul is more attuned to prose than to poetry; what he wants above all is sober reality, not fantasy!

Next to critical learning Boyle insists on "good judgment" for the study of Scripture. The ability to explain a text simply, as it was intended, instead of attributing all sorts of convoluted meanings to it, is often best exemplified, according to him, by non-theologians, like Grotius and Bacon, rather than by "commentators and other divines who, having espoused a church or party, and an aversion from all dissenters," are concerned, when they peruse Scripture, "to take notice chiefly of those things that may suggest either arguments against their adversaries or answers to their objections."[2] Boyle considers this a grave danger; he wants to go to Scripture without any theological axes to grind, and he indeed tries very hard to do so. Accordingly, he demands that isolated texts not be used to throw at each other like bricks, and that instead the structure of Scripture in its entirety be taken into account; this would silence many clamorous controversies, showing some to be groundless, and others undeterminable.[3] In short, we ought to "conform our opinions to the sense of Scripture [rather] than wrest the words of Scripture to them."[4]

Proceeding from this quintessentially Protestant principle, Boyle now places the confessions far below the Bible. In his opinion, far fewer articles of faith are absolutely necessary to be believed than are found in many lengthy confessions, while, conversely, a shorter confession like the Apostles' Creed ensures the possibility but not the certainty that it contains every fundamental article of the Christian faith.[5] Moreover, the confessions contain religion's *credenda* (what is to be believed), not its *agenda* (what is to be done).[6]

All this necessitates for Boyle a personal inquiry at the source. Why, he asks, should anyone who refuses to accept scientific and mathematical propositions without proof, accept the articles of faith, which concern matters of great and everlasting consequence, "upon the

---

[1] See my "Het Hypothesebegrip van Kepler," *Orgaan* (1939), p. 50.

[2] *The Excellency of Theology;* 4:17.

[3] *The Style of Holy Scripture*; 2:275.

[4] Ibidem.

[5] *The Excellency of Theology;* 4:25f. Think only of the notion so important to Reformed Christians, *sola fide,* by faith alone.

[6] Ibidem; 26.

authority of men fallible as themselves, when satisfaction may be had
without them from the infallible Word of God?"[1]

A certain latitude in exegesis, therefore, does not prevent him
from receiving the Bible as God's infallible Word. Accordingly, we do
not see him trying to deprive the miracle accounts of their historical
character; he accepts miracles for what they are whenever it appears to
him that this is what the writer intended. And although here too, as
everywhere else, he demands rationality, he also accepts what he
cannot rationally comprehend: in heaven we shall discover that the
"strange and peculiar as well as cryptical method and style of Scripture,
which often costs us so much study to find it rational," is worthy of its
omniscient Author; there we shall understand the meaning of the most
obscure and seemingly contradictory texts.[2]

Apparently, then, Boyle accepts the doctrine of inspiration unconditionally; his demand that Scripture be rational is not paramount.
He accepts Scripture, and accordingly supposes that it *must* be rational
in its deepest essence; and he does his best to discover this rationality.
Whenever that fails, it admonishes us to be humble, invites us to
veneration of the Supreme Reason, but never leads us to unbelief!

Not only is the Bible, according to Boyle, indispensable for coming to
a true faith, but it also contains a great deal which neither bare reason
nor philosophy can discover on its own strength, such as the genesis of
the world.[3]

Now it was common in Boyle's day to draw far-reaching scientific
conclusions from the Book of Genesis, to build on it a so-called Mosaic
philosophy.[4] This is by no means Boyle's intention. He declares that
he does not agree with those who deduce certain theorems of natural
philosophy from this or that expression in a book that was designed to
instruct us about spiritual rather than material things.[5] In this he stays
in tune with the Reformed tradition; Calvin likewise did not consider
Scripture a handbook for science.[6]

---

[1] *The Excellency of Theology*; 4:26.

[2] *Seraphic Love;* 1:289.

[3] *The Excellency of Theology;* 4:11.

[4] See my *Natuurwetenschap en Religie in het licht der historie,* p. 7 [and
Religion and the Rise of Modern Science (Edinburgh, 1972), chap. 5b].

[5] *The Excellency of Theology;* 4:11.

[6] "He who would learn astronomy and other occult sciences, let him go
elsewhere; . . . it is a book for the laity." John Calvin, *Commentary on
Genesis,* at Gen. 1:6. On Gen. 1:14 he writes: "It must be remembered that

This is no reason for Boyle, however, to turn Genesis 1 and 2 into an allegory[1] and to deny their literal and historical sense. Although Scripture is not given us for instruction in philosophical (read: scientific) truths, he writes, nevertheless Genesis contains all sorts of particulars about the origin of things which afford "very considerable hints" to science, albeit they may not serve there as sole arguments.[2]

The last clause points up once again that Boyle shrinks from drawing scientific conclusions from Bible texts and jealously guards the autonomy of science over against theology.

Inversely, he also guards against drawing from nature theological conclusions that go beyond a general sense of divinity. He does not, like Paracelsus, find the mystery of the Holy Trinity in a triadic division of macrocosm and microcosm,[3] nor is it a fruit of rational reflection, but it is a given through revelation in Holy Scripture.[4] Thus Boyle is much more modest with his "proofs" for the dogmas of Christianity than are some present-day theologians!

Neither is Boyle willing to draw the *theosophic* parallel between macrocosm and microcosm that we find, among others, in Paracelsus. The notion that man is an image of the world he rejects as contrary to Scripture, which teaches that man is created in the image of *God*.[5] He adopts a very sober attitude with regard to "chemical mysticism"[6] and condemns the theological digressions of the alchemists. Nor does he believe that they make their discoveries on the basis of "revelations." Indeed, many things are discovered "rather by accident than by accurate inquiries," and this God uses to keep the philosopher humble.[7]

Unquestionably it is a major principle of the Reformation to acknowledge Scripture as the sole authority in matters of faith, rather than the internal authority of the private sentiments of an individual, or

---

Moses is not philosophizing about occult mysteries but is referring to what are everywhere the elementary notions in use among the common people." On Gen. 1:16: "Here lies the difference: Moses wrote in a *popular* style about things that everybody endowed with common sense is able to understand."

[1] This was done shortly thereafter by the geologist Thomas Burnet; see Lechler, *Geschichte des englischen Deismus*, p. 123.

[2] *The Excellency of Theology;* 4:11.

[3] *Meteora*, cap. 2; cf. Huser's edition of Paracelsus' *Bücher und Schriften* (Basel, 1589–90), 8:186.

[4] *The Excellency of Theology;* 4:15.

[5] *The Usefulness of Natural Philosophy;* 2:54.

[6] Cf. my *Natuurwetenschap en Religie in het licht der historie,* pp. 4–7.

[7] *The Usefulness of Natural Philosophy;* 2:61f.

the external authority of an ecclesiastical teaching office. This special emphasis on the objective truth of Scripture is meant to oppose the enthusiasm of the sects and the heterodoxy of the Church. Yet no *break* with the Christian tradition is intended, only a *purification* of it.

However, the English Independentism that prevailed during the Commonwealth and continued to exert its influence thereafter also on Boyle and his kindred spirits, was a hyper-protestant phenomenon. Congregationalist in its view of the church, it had a strong biblicistic bent. Most Protestants of this persuasion, who, endowed with "good judgment," read Scripture in a straightforward manner, did arrive (thanks in part to the heritage of their forbears) at conclusions which the Church of all ages had always drawn. They accepted the great dogmas—Incarnation, Atonement, Redemption, Trinity, Free Grace—in the traditional sense.[1]

But there were also many among them who, equally sensible and of good judgment, without inclining to excesses, did come to deviating opinions. When the interpretation of the sole rule of faith, Scripture, is left entirely up to the individual person, it appears that one cannot help but acknowledge Christ as Savior and accept his death on the cross and his resurrection as historical facts; yet it appears as well that the intellect may so manage to interpret Scripture on the question of the deity of Christ and the Trinity that Arianism is the result. Thus Cromwell was orthodox as regards the Trinity, but his secretary Milton already entertained semi-Arian notions.[2] This rationalistic individualism is the reason why we meet with every shade of opinion, from orthodoxy according to the Nicene and Athanasian creeds, all the way to Unitarianism,[3] the beginnings of liberal Protestantism. From this one

---

[1] *Author's note for the English edition:* In this section "Puritanism" has been identified too much with the Independents (Congregationalists). There are also Anglican puritans. Cf. my paper "Puritanism and Science," Unit 6 in the series *Scientific Progress and Religious Dissent,* vol. 3 (Open University Press, 1974).

[2] Charles de Rémusat, *Histoire de la philosophie en Angleterre depuis Bacon jusqu'à Locke* (Paris, 1875), 1:98.

[3] Not just a rationalist "independent" inquiry of the Bible can give rise to deviating opinions; depending on whether intellect or feeling predominates, liberalism or enthusiasm may result. Both rest on a "truth within us"; both make man sovereign. It is often noted that "fanatical" sects exhibit strong rationalistic features: the Brethren of the Free Spirit, Anabaptists, Dutch Mennonites! What has further led to fragmentation is the fact that Puritan biblicism insists on a literal precept in the Bible for everything (think of Sunday observance!). Thus it generated the Baptist movement, which rejects

slides further down the slope, toward deism,[1] for between a "Christian theism" and every other purified monotheism there is no profound difference of principle.

Nonetheless Boyle is still of the conviction that a right use of reason will lead as a matter of course to the orthodox position. Like most Englishmen, he has a naive faith in "common sense." It is his view that if a text allows of two interpretations, the "most rational" one should be chosen! That is indeed a wise rule, but it may also make a person feel he or she has the right to a "rational" conception of the Trinity, or of the two natures of Christ, instead of the supra-rational one of the Church.

This is not the case with Boyle, however. He states that when the Bible speaks of things that the natural understanding must be silent about, the latter will nevertheless have to accept the truth of Scripture. But not everyone will agree with this; besides, who draws the boundary between the rational and the supra-rational? Boyle's view comes down to this, that the truth of Scripture stands firm and is afterwards interpreted as rationally as possible. He says himself that since the Bible always turns out to be so truthful and rational he is willing to believe it unconditionally regarding those much "darker" doctrines which (like the Trinity) utterly surpass the understanding.[2]

Boyle accepts the Incarnation, the Trinity, the doctrine of free grace, and the other great dogmas unconditionally.[3] His study of the Bible never causes him to deviate from them. He gladly accepts everything taught by the church he is most attached to. He is a convinced Anglican and subscribes wholeheartedly to the Thirty-nine Articles,[4] even while he knows of others who likewise acknowledge Scripture to be the Word of God yet who arrive at strongly divergent views. But this does not disturb him in the least; he is convinced that God reveals himself clearly and unmistakably insofar as this is

---

infant baptism because it is not clearly taught in Scripture, and Seventh-Day Adventism, which finds prescribed in Scripture not the celebration of Sunday but of the Sabbath.

[1] Rémusat, *Histoire de la philosophie en Angleterre*, p. 92.

[2] The doctrine of the Trinity, however, is not against reason but above reason; this was also Tillotson's view against the Socinians; cf. Lechler, *Geschichte des englischen Deismus*, p. 147.

[3] *Seraphic Love;* 1:266–69.

[4] "He did thoroughly agree with the doctrines of our church, and conform to our worship," writes Bishop Burnet; *Life;* 1:cxli.

necessary for salvation; should anything give rise to different interpretations among "sensible" people, it cannot be of any consequence.

Among the Puritans, a difference in interpretation led quickly to the formation of a new sect; not so among the faithful of Boyle's type, who will generally regard any difference, should it arise, as of secondary importance and therefore not worth breaking the unity over. They aspire after a church of Bible believers: when Boyle defends the "possibility" of the bodily resurrection of Christ, he is not concerned with all the things that any particular church or sect may have taught about the resurrection ("I declare myself to be unconcerned to defend them") but only with "what is plainly taught about it in the holy scriptures themselves."[1] He is convinced that by less theologizing about Scripture and more personal searching after the truths of Scripture, and, above all, by a "conforming of our lives to our discoveries," we may miss a great many theological truths, but not salvation.[2]

b. The Confessions

Boyle's views on ecclesiastical policy are those of the Comprehension. He is tolerant with respect to those of other minds. Among his correspondents we encounter Presbyterians, Independents, and even Quakers (for example, William Penn). He is strongly opposed to all religious persecution[3] and refuses to make an issue of church polity which was just then so hotly under debate in England. In 1647, thus at the outset of the Commonwealth, he writes that during his stay in Geneva the people seemed quite content with a church government whose intolerable yoke is the "grand scare-crow that frights us here," yet neither is it of such transcendent excellency that he would "bolt heaven against, or open Newgate [prison!] for, all those who believe they may be saved under another."[4] Even the most fanatical sects he would not want to see opposed by the strong arm of the law: "As for our upstart sectaries, which rise from the ground like mushrooms: the worst will decay as suddenly as they sprang up, like Jonah's gourd, smitten at the root with the worm of their irrationality." The safest way to destroy them is not to kill them, but to let them die of themselves.[5] Boyle's confidence in the triumph of reason is again remarkable.

---

[1] *The Possibility of the Resurrection;* 4:192f.
[2] *Life;* 1:xlix.
[3] Ibidem; cxli.
[4] Ibidem; xl.
[5] Ibidem.

This is not to say, however, that he looked at the fragmentation of the church with indifference. On the contrary, comprehension implied a strong desire for unity. He could not help but see that Protestantism ran the danger of foundering on internal divisions, and as early as 1646 he complains that in London at least one sect is born every day, and that whoever has lost his religion can always find another one in London but whoever would save his religion runs the danger of losing it in London.[1]

In 1647 he writes to John Dury, who had made attempts at reconciling Calvinists and Lutherans, that it saddens him "to see such comparatively petty differences in judgment make such wide breaches and vast divisions in affection." He finds it strange that men "should rather be quarrelling for a few trifling opinions wherein they dissent than to embrace one another for those many fundamental truths wherein they agree."[2] Meanwhile, "the great and the most important, as well as most universally acknowledged truths were by all sides almost as generally neglected as they were confessed."[3]

His aversion to divisions among Christians is apparent even from beyond the grave. In his last will and testament Boyle left a fixed sum for defraying the costs of an annual lecture series for the defense of the Christian religion, the defense to be directed "against notorious Infidels, *viz.* Atheists, Theists [i.e., deists], Pagans, Jews, and Mahometans, *not descending lower to any controversies that are among Christians themselves.*"[4]

Boyle held fast to the obligation to preserve unity and he remained faithful to the Established Church, even though he had a few objections. In spite of his charitable attitude toward the dissenters he never visited their meetings.[5]

Thus he was not so much vexed by the differences of opinion as by the fact that this led to new denominations. In this he showed himself to be a "latitudinarian," a true Anglican of the Broad Church which aimed at embracing all nuances in one church organization and under one form of liturgy.

Boyle and his circle of friends shared the attitude of the bishops under William III, who, loyal to the Established Church, strove after a reconciliation with the dissenters (short of Unitarians and Socinians,

---

[1] Ibidem; xxxv.

[2] Ibidem; xxxix.

[3] Ibidem; cxli.

[4] Ibidem; clxvii; emphasis added.

[5] Ibidem; cxl.

who were clearly heretical) and after a unity of faith based on the fundamental principles of orthodoxy. This was the circle from which emerged the Edict of Toleration, the "broad" but not "deep" orthodoxy of the Church of England with its aversion to an elaborate dogmatical system and to romanization. It is a church which in its further development, for all its tendency toward "reasonableness," has an aversion to avowed modernism[1] yet tolerates that one has his own mind about the most orthodox formulations in confessions and liturgy! This is an orthodoxy which, although originally of the Calvinist variety, abhors pronouncements that are too shocking to the intellect or the emotions and which therefore often leans toward Arminianism. Episcopius, the well-known Arminian theologian, was very influential in England; Boyle too had a high estimate of him. But like most English theologians of otherwise unimpeachable orthodoxy, Boyle does not openly express his sympathy for the Dutch Arminians, even though it was evidently not quite on the side of Dordt either!

Boyle accepts completely what the Bible says about God's free grace; in this he takes the standpoint of Articles 10 and 17 of the Anglican confession.[2] God, according to him, grants his grace unconditionally, according to his own choosing, and absolutely not according to our merit; he therefore has an eternal decree of election or reprobation in relation to every human being.[3] Although God takes pleasure in our good works, they are not the cause of his love.[4]

Nevertheless Boyle declines to give his opinion "concerning the controversies betwixt the Calvinists and the Remonstrants about predestination." The one wishes more to celebrate God's justice, the other God's goodness; the one believes grace to be irresistible, the other holds that it will make every man happy *if he pleases.* Yet the Calvinist doctrine of predestination, according to Boyle, is rejected by "the Lutherans and diverse learned divines of the Church of England." To "justify the freeness of God's love" does not require it; "the dispute

---

[1] Dr. E. W. Barnes, the current [1943] bishop of Birmingham, is generating much offense by his open and aggressive modernism, although his attitude reaps greater sympathy than that of some High Churchmen who are to all intents and purposes theological modernists but who manage better to maintain decorum.

[2] Art. 10: "Of free will"; art. 17: "Of Predestination and Election"; both Calvinist in substance. One can find them in the back of the Book of Common Prayer.

[3] *Seraphic Love;* 1:277.

[4] Ibidem; 273.

betwixt the Calvinists and Arminians is not so much concerning the
thing, as concerning the manner of its being proffered": for even the
power to accept grace is given by God; according to the Remonstrants,
man need merely "not wilfully refuse it."[1]

Apparently Boyle wants to remain completely in tune with the
Bible and has the vague feeling that the Arminians could do with some
defense. He points out that the Remonstrant confession expressly
mentions the freedom and unmeritedness of God's grace. He shies
away from the crass formulations of the Counter-Remonstrants,
however, as he fears they may give rise to laxness of morals[2]—and
passiveness in matters of faith certainly does not comport well with the
Anglo-Saxon spirit. Incidentally, that sentimentality plays no role here
becomes evident when he says that "hell's darkness doth as well
contribute to God's glory as heaven's eternal splendor."[3]

Arminian influence may account as well for Boyle's view that no
elaborate confession binding on everyone is required, but only a few
cardinal points.

The Scottish theologian Halyburton writes: "The Dutch [Remon-
strant] doctrine that only those few articles are essential which everyone
confesses, must lead to deism, for what article is not contested?"[4] This
critic has hit the nail on the head. If reason becomes the only judge in
matters of faith, it will become apparent that even the most seemingly
unequivocal Scripture passages may give rise to the most divergent
interpretations. Left entirely free, many will choose for a synthesis
between Faith and Reason that derogates least from human nature.
History has shown that higher criticism undermines the authority of
Scripture, and that a biblicistic Protestantism easily fades away into a
rationalistic monotheism. The sovereignty of the individual Christian
leads in the long run to a self-willed religion that is far removed from
what is still paramount in Boyle, namely the acknowledgment of
Scripture as the infallible revelation of God.

In appealing to reason as a safeguard against error, Boyle
overlooks that it is *the faith of the believing community* that has
safeguarded him (and every Protestant in love with freedom of inquiry)
from the errors of reason itself. His "rational religion" passes over the
mystical character of faith, which surely attests, "I can do no other, for
my spirit testifies with God's Spirit that this is the truth."

---

[1] Ibidem; 277f.
[2] Ibidem; 277.
[3] Ibidem; 272.
[4] Quoted in Rémusat, *Histoire de la philosophie en Angleterre*, p. 96.

The Reformed churches, too, have followed an undefined tradition and held fast to the unity of believers since apostolic times. They have carefully weighed the pronouncements of the ancient church, of the fathers, of synods, of the reformers; they have tested them once more against Scripture, and they have been quite content, where Scripture does not seem clear, to accept the interpretation of the ancients. While he does not openly admit it, in Boyle too we see reason only go so far as is in keeping with traditional Christian belief. Although, like a true Protestant, he does not place the old symbols above or alongside Scripture as an *authority,* still they serve him as a guide in expounding Scripture; in fact, even the Thirty-nine Articles contribute to the guidelines that govern his Bible study.[1] Boyle's "simple faith" is enriched by the faith of all ages, by the treasures from the history of the Church.

How then are we to explain in Boyle, who surely wants to be anything but "Independent," that ardent defense of *sola Scriptura?* Through his evangelical piety and strict morality he has greater affinity with the Low Church and the dissenters than with the formalistic orthodoxy of many Restoration bishops in whom High Church loyalty is coupled with religious indifference. He notices how in those circles the Church's doctrine (as it lies ready in summary form in the Confession) is merely affirmed without ever coming to personal assent, in order to be rid of the need of personal inquiry. This love of ease is characteristic, according to Boyle, also of many naturalists. It is in Hobbes that this attitude with respect to religion finds its philosophical and barefaced expression: the prince determines what is true in religion.[2]

But still another danger threatens. Under protection from James, the brother of Charles II, the papists are rearing their heads, and that spells to the Englishman increased influence for Louis XIV, hence even

---

[1] The Anglican confession considers Scripture sufficient (Art. 6) yet states emphatically that the three ancient creeds "ought thoroughly to be received and believed; for they may be proved by most certain warrants of Holy Scripture" (Art. 8).

[2] Hobbes was one of the few men in regard to whom Boyle openly showed his annoyance, however mild-tempered he might otherwise be. Hobbes, however, touched him on two tender spots: he ridiculed the experimental research of the Royal Society, and in his *Leviathan* he proclaimed "dangerous opinions about some very important, if not fundamental, articles of religion"; the book *Leviathan,* according to Boyle, had made "but too great impressions" upon certain persons who possess more status than wisdom. *Against Hobbes;* 1:187.

greater intolerance and frivolity. Although Boyle adopts a mild attitude also toward Roman Catholics, he is too consciously Protestant than that he would be religiously indifferent to romanization.[1] In 1680 he underwrites the publication of Gilbert Burnet's *History of the Reformation*. The fundamental principles of the Reformation must be preserved and in order to stand firm it is necessary that everyone read the Bible for himself; in 1665 he writes his plea for personal Bible study. Too much is at stake for him than that the responsibility for what to believe may be left to others: Why should anyone "take up the articles of faith, concerning matters of great and everlasting consequence, upon the authority of men, fallible as themselves, when satisfaction may be had without them from the infallible word of God?"[2]

Accordingly, Boyle emphasizes the fundamental fallibility of every human formulation of faith. As he does so, he accepts the Bible without

---

[1] Already on his journey through France and Italy in 1641 Boyle did not receive a favorable impression of Catholicism. He was not surprised that the pope forbade Protestants access to Rome, since "nothing could more affirm them in their religion" than a visit to that city. *Life*; 1:xxv.

After 1660 the alarm about romanization among Boyle's friends grew steadily, especially after James II had begun his reign. It is amusing to read about this in the letters of the bishop of Lincoln, Thomas Barlow, a great patristic scholar, a vehement opponent of the persecution of dissenters, one of Boyle's closest friends. The bishop, although nearly 80, appears to be of a fierier temper than the grave Boyle. He keeps Boyle informed of the "old gentleman at Rome" (the pope) and his party in England, which he (Barlow) has challenged in a pamphlet. For this they will probably anathematize him "with bell, book and candle" and damn him as a desperate heretic, but they do not frighten him, "nor shall I think myself less catholic because they call me (what they really are) an heretic." Notwithstanding any danger the future might hold for him, Barlow writes on 7 April 1684, he is not afraid to stand by what he has written. *Letters;* 6:307. Apparently the bishop knew what he could expect from someone like James! Boyle answers that he is glad the bishop is willing to close the gap which, if left open, will probably widen more and more and prove "an inlet to innovations dangerous to the church of England, and consequently to the protestant cause"; having lived in several popish countries, Boyle expects more danger than benefit from the introduction of images in churches. Ibidem; 6:313. In July 1687 Barlow writes about further attempts at popish infiltration. However, he feels reassured, for many prophecies indicate that "Babylon must fall . . . the very next year 1688." Ibidem; 6:319. Indeed, the accession in 1689 of Mary and William (the champion of the Protestant religion) ushered in a golden age for Boyle's friends!

[2] *The Excellency of Theology;* 4:26.

reservation as God's infallible revelation; among Christians in those days that standpoint did not yet need any defense. He recognizes the difficulty that this infallible Word is read and interpreted by fallible people, for he writes that one should not place one's confidence in others, though he forgets to mention that one should place one's confidence as little in oneself. Boyle expects too much from the human mind; like many of his contemporaries he looks forward to enlightenment in the future. He does not accentuate the standpoint of faith that it is the Spirit who leads the Church into all truth.

§ 4. The Nature of Boyle's Faith

Boyle's religion, like his science, has an empiricist and a rationalist element; as in science, he puts the emphasis on the former. "We know a revelation through testimony, not through ratiocination." Seen from that standpoint, even his "natural religion" is a revealed religion, for it rests upon the revelation of God in nature. This revelation, however, is accessible to every sensible man. What we lack here is a difference of level between revelation in nature and special revelation; the latter seems a supplement, on a par with natural knowledge. As an experiment cuts the knot when reason hesitates between two hypotheses, so special revelation decides, for example, in the matter of the immortality of the soul. Boyle's argument fails to reflect the fact that the acceptance of special revelation (Scripture) requires a special grace, just as general revelation in nature is accepted by a general or common grace. Nature and Scripture are for him equally accessible to all men; whoever will use his reason aright can investigate and accept both. If natural religion in Boyle is to a certain extent a revealed religion, his revealed religion is in a certain sense a natural religion.

But does Boyle in this way ever get beyond a "historical" faith? It seems as though he dislikes alluding to election, even though he accepts it,[1] so that we almost get the impression that he is content with a faith of that kind.

It is unquestionably a point in his favor that he considers the certainty of religion in no way inferior to the certainty of science, but still there is something suspicious about that near identification. Granted, he curtails the pride both of science and of all human, natural theology, and he demonstrates that neither science nor religion is entirely rational; but he views this deficiency as of the same type and attributes it too much to the finite nature of the human understanding

[1] *Seraphic Love;* 1:277.

alone. He does not sufficiently bring out the difference in character between science and religion: the place that Experience and Reason have in the one they have also in the other, making both appear to fall within the sphere of common grace. Boyle's view of religion is lacking in the Christian notion that it is in religion that the "enmity" between God and man is brought into strong relief.

If Nature and Scripture are regarded by him perhaps too much as empirical data of the same kind, no less does reason play an analogous role in assimilating what they reveal. Reason, though it falls short in science and in natural theology, does recognize that the Christian revelation is the true one, even though it does so *a posteriori;* and reason does acknowledge that certain things in revelation have to be accepted even if they surpass the human understanding. When all is said and done, does this religion, for all its qualifications, not end up becoming a rationalistic religion after all? Is it man who through his reason comes to God, or does God come to man? What has happened to the divine activity in conversion?

It is noteworthy that Boyle makes so little mention of grace, even though he must have realized, on the basis of the confessions he embraced wholeheartedly, and on the basis of the Scriptures he loved so much, that that is where the heart of the matter lies. But we must not forget that we know only apologetic works of Boyle, addressed to intellectual outsiders. In these he must necessarily approach faith from the side of man and try to make the intellect or the will come round to his position. The acknowledgment that "grace" is at work here holds only for those who are already believers. Nor must we overlook that Boyle was very reserved when it came to expressing his innermost feelings, even in his letters. The "unpublished" fragment of his autobiography shows, however, that he had a profound sense of God.

For that matter, Boyle's information to his readers is one-sided. Apart from the concept of God that must naturally transcend all understanding, many "mysteries" remain (such as the Trinity, the Incarnation), which he is happy to believe because the Christian revelation appears so rational everywhere else. But his intellect could not have *forced* him to do that; he must have *willed* it. He puts the intellect above the will, but in reality it was his *will* that drove him to embrace the faith. Recurring doubt compelled him to give an account to himself of his faith on "rational" grounds. That doubt he considered a "temptation," a "disease to his faith." He never lost this faith, not even when he doubted it. That doubt brought him to such despair that he would have taken his own life if . . . his faith had not forbidden it! From the human side, therefore, his conversion was more a process of the will than an intellectual process. From the other side, he himself acknowledged election and the operation of grace, for the core of his forthright confession is that Christ, "who long had lain asleep in his conscience," awoke, and God restored unto him "the withdrawn sense of his favour" (after partaking of the means of *grace:* the Lord's supper!).[1] Here it is clear that faith was more for him than a mere intellectual matter; it was also a personal relationship with God. His apologetic works may all be addressed to the intellect, but Boyle must have been very much aware that in this way he could only instil an intellectual conviction, an "historical" faith—that he could *convince* but not *convert,* or, as he put it, that "to convince them is not enough to convert them," and that a conversion of the inward man is the work of divine grace.

§ 5. Boyle and Pascal as Apologists

Boyle and Pascal were both prominent practitioners of science and earnest Christians who put religion above science. Pascal solved mathematical problems to show the "world" that a "converted" too knows how to use his natural gifts. Boyle would rather have all his other works unread than see his religious works forgotten.

Both men lived in a similar milieu. Pascal faced the scepticism and frivolity of the France of Louis XIV; loose morals and worldliness went hand in hand with ritualism and Jesuit formalism. Boyle's greatest activity fell in the "merry reign" of Charles II. Here too religious indifference went hand in hand with immorality, while the episcopal clergy persecuted the "Puritan fanaticks" with a passion matched only by the vehemence of the Jesuits against the Jansenists. Pascal, however, participated in the struggle with great fervor; Boyle kept his distance and combated the evil more than the evil-doers.

The two have in common their Christian realism. In science they oppose an *a priori* system; they want to accept the creation, not as we might wish it, but as God gave it. Boyle writes, "Geometry, or revelation, or experience, assure us of divers things of which we can know but that they are and what they do, not what they are and how they act."[2] Pascal too is compelled, as he contemplates nature, man and God, to acknowledge that there are *real* things in science, mathematics and theology that surpass our understanding, and he comes to declare, "It is not by our capacity to conceive things that we should judge of

---

[1] *Life;* 1:xxiii.
[2] *Things Above Reason;* 4:447.

their truth,"[1] and to write, "Not all that is incomprehensible ceases to exist: infinite number."[2]

Methodologically, both men keep their science and religion strictly separate, lest unwarranted mixing occur. Yet the works of both make plain that there is a close connection between religious persuasion and scientific work.

In Boyle and Pascal we find a pronounced scientific empiricism, yet also—and here Descartes, whom they both take issue with, is certainly influential—a strong rationalism. The "stupefaction" that a skillful and intelligent contemplation of nature instills in men is counted by Boyle among the *rational* forms of veneration of the Creator,[3] and Pascal time and again uses reason to humble Reason.

Their theology too is empirical; they cherish the absolute authority of Scripture because Scripture reflects reality: it depicts man in such a way that everyone has to admit: that is how he is. In consequence, both men bring into prominence the historical nature of the Christian faith; they derive proofs from fulfilled prophecies.

Yet, despite all resemblance, what a difference! We have already pointed this out when discussing their scientific methodology, but it is starkly apparent in their apologetic method as well.

Pascal does not, like Boyle, look for a synthesis between faith and science. Once he fully shares in the faith he abandons science, whereas Boyle continues to be engaged in it right into old age. In Pascal there is a compact between *scepticism* and religion. He takes a grim delight in using reason to show up its insufficiency in science and morality. In Boyle, by contrast, there is an alliance between *reason* and religion. He states apologetically, when pointing out the insufficiency of reason, that he in no way wants to disparage it; he seems to be taking the first step toward that typically English variety of Christianity, "that comfortable Christianity which demands no sacrifice of the proud intellect."[4]

Boyle attacks the scepticism which during the Restoration was undermining faith, science and morality; he is exceedingly annoyed by Hobbes, who says that every man is a wolf to his fellow-man. Pascal would have turned this statement to his advantage; he takes the scepticism of his day as a starting-point for apologetics. That is not just a question of tactics: the consequences of the Fall in their effect on

---

[1] *De l'esprit géométrique*, Harvard Classics ed. (1910), p. 439.

[2] *Pensées*, nr. 430.

[3] *The Veneration Owed to God;* 5:132.

[4] Rémusat, *Histoire de la philosophie en Angleterre,* p. 96.

intellect and will, on science and morality, go much deeper for Pascal than for Boyle. He puts far more emphasis on the fact that man's *will* has been corrupted; consequently, his apologetics addresses the *heart* much more than the intellect.[1]

By contrast, Boyle, who regards the intellect as a higher attribute of the mind than the will, addresses the intellect more than the heart. Intellectual objections he tries to meet intellectually. Nevertheless he knows that, even though the intellect may be forced to acknowledge that the Christian standpoint is correct, the will does not surrender so easily. However, he takes that to be obstinacy. It is striking, therefore, that Pascal attempts to rob man of *all* his certainty, to demonstrate his corruption and imperfection in intellect (science) and will (morality); the sceptic Montaigne provides him with arguments in abundance. Boyle, however, is far removed from scepticism; he shows "sensible men of good will" that Christianity is a "rational" religion. Boyle says: Use your understanding! Pascal would like to get man to pray: Incline mine heart![2]

The purpose of apologetics with Boyle is above all to justify revelation *a posteriori* through a broad selection of arguments; with Pascal it is to confront man through inexorable logic with the dilemma that *this* is the answer or there is *no* answer. Pascal is deeper but less broad than Boyle.

It is not the case that Pascal denies all revelation in nature or that he denies the natural moral law, while it is equally true, on the other hand, that Boyle acknowledges their insufficiency and lets mystery be mystery. But Pascal has more of an eye for God's hiddenness in nature, whereas Boyle sees in nature the self-revealing God. Hence Boyle's preference for the teleological argument, while Pascal is more quick to note the want of design in nature and declines to derive positive arguments from it since he reckons the consequences of the Fall too great for that.[3] He does not believe that the world exists to give positive instruction, but only to disabuse us of our innocence. He wants to lead man to revealed religion by demonstrating that natural theology is uncertain: the world shows "neither a total exclusion nor a manifest presence of divinity."[4] He feels that what we gain by natural theology

---

[1] Cf. my "Pascal, His Science and His Religion," *Tractrix* 1 (1989): 138.

[2] [Cf. *Pensées,* nrs. 252, 284, quoting Ps. 119:36.]

[3] *Pensées,* nrs. 242, 244, 248, 556.

[4] Ibidem, nr. 556.

we lose again—unless we submit to Christ—by our pride in it![1] Far more than our own insight, which makes us think so easily that we have come to God of ourselves, he emphasizes grace: "lest the cross of Christ be made of none effect."[2]

Pascal shows the uncertainty of the foundations of sovereign science, sovereign morality and sovereign religion, to make room for faith; he believes that science, philosophy, morality and religion are relatively indifferent so long as the fixed standpoint is wanting—so long as there is no unconditional surrender to God's revelation in Christ. For Boyle, however, they are not *uncertain* so much as *insufficient;* he does not, like Pascal, see their impotence, but their insufficiency; they are not supplanted but supplemented by divine revelation. Natural religion for Boyle is an introduction to revealed religion; unlike Pascal, he does not criticize its content but only its scope, and in a positive way he makes it serviceable to faith.

In sum: Boyle and Pascal faced the same adversaries, the *beaux esprits,* the school-philosophers, atheists and deists; but Boyle had in addition to contend with those who (be they religious or irreligious) denied the usefulness of science!

Pascal is more an apologist for twentieth-century man, Boyle for man of the nineteenth century. Pascal comes close to the motto *credo quia absurdum:* "I believe because it is absurd"; Boyle's position echoes the slogan *fides quaerit intellectum:* "faith seeks understanding."

Standing before his Maker, Pascal is especially impressed by his awesome majesty, Boyle by his wisdom and goodness. The passion with which Pascal surrenders to Jesus runs much deeper than the calm, rational sentiment of gratitude felt by Boyle. Blaise Pascal's writings, comparatively few in number but penetrating, pithy, passionate, make a bigger impression than the effusiveness with which the solemn periods roll down the several thousand pages of the folio volumes of the Works of Robert Boyle.

While Pascal remains uncertain in the face of creation and is so impressed by the numinous that it dampens his genuine *joy* in it, Boyle's attitude toward nature is one of cheerful embrace. True, he lacks the spontaneous and jubilant elements so charming in Kepler. Boyle is much more formal and prosaic in his glorification of the work of God's Fingers. Nevertheless, in his case too, a fruitful engagement of science was not hampered but promoted by the Christian faith.

---

[1] Ibidem, nr. 543; cf. nr. 556: "such knowledge without Jesus Christ is useless and barren."

[2] Ibidem, nr. 245, quoting I Cor. 1:17.

INDEX OF NAMES

GENERAL THEOLOGICAL SEMINARY
NEW YORK